Studies in Writing & Rhetoric

Other Books in the Studies in Writing & Rhetoric Series

Revisionary Rhetoric, Feminist Pedagogy, and Multigenre Texts

Revisionary Rhetoric, Feminist Pedagogy, and Multigenre Texts

[handwritten inscription:] To Kirstin, my favorite Illinois poet — who inspires me to dream BIG, to go in search of all my possible drafts. With love & gratitude!

Julie Jung

[signature]

SOUTHERN ILLINOIS UNIVERSITY PRESS

Carbondale

Publication partially funded by a subvention grant from The Conference on College
Composition and Communication of the National Council of Teachers of English.

Library of Congress Cataloging-in-Publication Data
Jung, Julie, 1966–
Revisionary rhetoric, feminist pedagogy, and multigenre texts / Julie Jung.
   p. cm. — (Studies in writing & rhetoric)
Includes bibliographical references and index.
1. English language—Rhetoric—Study and teaching. 2. Report writing—Study
and teaching (Higher). 3. Feminism and education. 4. Literary form. I. Title.
II. Series.
PE1404.J86 2005
808'.042'0711—dc22   2004023937
ISBN 0-8093-2610-8 (pbk. : alk. paper)

Printed on recycled paper. ♻

The paper used in this publication meets the minimum requirements of American
National Standard for Information Sciences—Permanence of Paper for Printed
Library Materials, ANSI Z39.48-1992. ∞

*For my mom, Marge Kolb,
and my first grade teacher,
Nancy Hartzell,
both of whom taught me how
to read and write,
and for Tilly Warnock
who taught me how to read
and write—again*

Contents

Preface

> Hence, I concluded that trouble is inevitable and the task, how
> best to make it, what best way to be in it.
>
> —Judith Butler

For most of my life, I have been energized intellectually and personally by the disruptions that result when I put two "wrong" things together. In the second grade, I caused a food fight in the school cafeteria when I sat on the boys' side at lunch. In high school I organized a football game between the students who hung out in the smoking area (the freaks) and those in the National Honors Society (the nerds). Later I confused everyone by pursuing graduate degrees in English after earning a bachelor of arts in math. For me, though, these actions weren't confusing; rather, they provided me with an experiential knowledge base that has motivated much of my scholarly work—the knowledge that disrupting expectations can result in expanded and revised points of view, that from such disruptions one can develop the epistemological pliancy one needs to negotiate responsibly an ever-changing world.

While it is true that part of me loves to cause trouble, to disrupt what people have come to expect, another part of me resists my penchant for troublemaking with everything she's got. From as early as I can remember, a voice inside me has asked the same two questions: "Why do you have to be so weird? Why can't you just fit in?" When the popular girls in my seventh-grade class asked me to join their clique, I said no, because I knew belonging to their group meant I could no longer play with Lisa, who was teaching me to mime and who was rewriting canonical plays I'd never even heard of. I loved playing with Lisa, who was brilliant and odd, but I still cried when invitations to the biggest parties didn't get sent to me. I didn't want to be boxed in, but I didn't want to be rejected, either.

This same push-pull of competing desires—the impulse to push against established boundaries, the yearning to fit comfortably within them—plays out every day of my life. I know now that I was drawn to rhetoric and composition studies because it didn't box me in. It allowed me to muck around in different disciplines, texts, and contexts. In fact, it expected me to. I was a math nerd who loved to write, and I felt welcomed. And yet, despite the roominess of my adopted discipline, I still longed for one that didn't demand so much explanation. "What's rhetoric?" family members asked, and each time I answered differently. "How do you teach someone to write?" friends in other fields inquired sincerely, and I shrugged, "I wish I knew."

In many ways, this book is an attempt to transform a private competition into a public collaboration, to sustain these competing desires long enough so that I and others like me can learn from them. In particular, my goal is to contribute to an ongoing project of retheorizing what it might mean to practice revision in various related contexts—the academic essay, the discipline of rhetoric and composition studies, the subfield of feminist composition, and the English studies classroom. My hope is that such a retheorizing will help us create an expansive revisionary space, one where we can both disrupt disciplinary expectations *and* not be rejected for doing so.

In chapter 1, "Writing That Listens: Defining Revisionary Rhetoric," I begin by questioning accepted wisdom regarding the purpose of revision—namely, to make meaning more clear. Using current theories of knowledge-making to critique existing theories and practices of revision, I follow Nancy Welch's (*Getting Restless*) lead and ask: What possible knowledges are lost when revision is theorized as a process of moving toward greater clarity of meaning or as negotiating consensus between writers and readers? How might contemporary feminist rhetorical theories, which emphasize the urgency of building alliances across fields of difference, be used to develop a theory of revision that recognizes the value of disruption in working toward greater understanding? In a classic troublemaking move, I then attempt to demonstrate the usefulness of theorizing revision in terms that run directly counter to the norm: to think of it as a process of *disrupting textual clarity* and thereby delaying consensus so that differences and conflicts within discourse communities can be identified, sustained, contended with, and perhaps understood.

The remaining chapters alternately celebrate how multigenre texts can practice this disruptive theory of revision, which I call revisionary rhetoric, as well as lament the loss of old terms of belonging. In chapter 2, "Do I Belong 'in' RhetComp: Revision, Identity, and Multigenre Texts," for example, I introduce the multigenre essay as a textual form that can problematize what it means to be a "RhetComp person," a moniker I heard repeatedly applied to me after beginning my first assistant professor job. Despite the fact that I *had* been hired specifically in a rhetoric and composition line, the label made me profoundly uncomfortable, leading me to ask: What are my colleagues assuming when they say and hear "RhetComp person"? How might I disrupt the belief that a "RhetComp person" is someone who is not "in" (and therefore in some ways *opposed to*) literature and creative writing? Pursuing these questions, I offer the multigenre text as an example of an inherently disruptive and therefore potentially revisionary written form, a kind of writing that brings together previously divided genres within the frame of a single academic essay. By refusing to "fit in" to the conventions of any one genre or subfield, and yet by building alliances with several different genres at once, multigenre texts demand new and better kinds of listening. Furthermore, because genre is inextricably tied to the construction of social identity (Bawarshi 353), and because multigenre texts juxtapose more than one genre, they can be studied to enhance our understanding of identity (dis/re)formation.[1] For example, how might the discomfort produced by genre switching promote the revisioning of prior expectations, the ways we have grown used to pigeonholing ourselves and others? How might the writing, reading, and teaching of multigenre texts challenge scholar-teachers' allegiances to a dominant RhetComp identity? What *is* this identity, and what rhetorical strategies are available to those who want to revise it?

In chapter 3, the context for examining the revisionary potential of multigenre texts shifts from published scholarship to the classroom. In "Putting the Wrongs Words Together: Disrupting Narratives in English Studies," I explore the pedagogical usefulness of assigning multigenre essays. More generally, this chapter addresses a frustration faced by many writing teachers: How can we get students to experience revision as an opportunity to see a subject anew rather than as a chore or, even worse, an indication of failure? Exemplifying one solution, I describe a multigenre essay assignment where students reflected on their semesterly experiences by incorporating and migrating to different genres produced in and out of school. In an analysis of two illustrative student essays, I discuss how these writers use genre migrations to construct different and sometimes contradictory subject positions as English majors and how their ability to contend with rather than ignore these differences generated a revised and deeper way of knowing. Additionally, because these students' arguments forced a revisioning of my identity as a teacher, I explore how the identities of RhetComp teachers might be affected when students juxtapose different genres within a single text. What tensions and resistances—personal and departmental—emerge when those who teach rhetoric and composition invite students to write in genres typically cordoned off to literature and creative writing classes?

In chapters 4 and 5, my interest in deploying multigenre texts to push against the constraints of a RhetComp identity—both as teacher and scholar—deepens, as I intersect the RhetComp moniker with another, equally troubling label: feminist. As a minimalist with a penchant for pricey shoes, a social constructionist who understands the appeal of a woodsy garret, I am deeply troubled by the pressures I feel to be a "good" feminist. In graduate school, my good friend and colleague, Melody Bowdon, and I somewhat jokingly founded The Bad Feminists Club, thereby giving ourselves permission to say and do things we would never say and do while among the discipline's most famous feminists. Thus far in my career, the pendulum of my competing desires has swung far to the side of belonging; I'd rather remain silent than risk losing membership in a community I feel I need in order to be happy in this profession. So, I take it as a healthy sign that I am now willing to identify and push against boundaries that I perceive as boxing me in. Specifically, I am troubled by the image I conjure when I hear "feminist compositionist"—that of a woman embittered by years of disrespect, even abuse, in a male-dominated, literature-heavy English department.[2]

This construct is, of course, the very real consequence of historical realities that have been well documented in our discipline, and while I am no doubt indebted to the women who survived that disrespect and abuse, thereby making life a lot easier for me, I want something else. I want to *like* literature and the people who teach it. I want to appreciate the canon even as I continue to work to revise it. I want to understand the poetry of solitary musing without dismissing it as expressivist crap or romantic privilege.

In short, I want more room. In an effort to make it, I examine how the multigenre essay can disrupt some of feminist composition's most tenacious binaries: process/product, mother/bitch, ethic of care/agonistic debate. For example, in chapter 4, "Toward Hearing the Impossible: A Multigenre Revision of Robert Connors's 'Teaching and Learning as a Man'—Revised," I analyze my initial and revised responses to Connors's (in)famous essay, focusing on the way my ability to respond was both created and limited by the traditional generic form Connors deploys. Troubled by my initial reading, which was angrily dismissive and therefore, in my mind, "properly" feminist, I worked harder to hear more fully Connors's argument, interviewing male writing teachers to learn about their experiences teaching male students. I offer the results of this research in the form of a multigenre, multivocal revision of Connors's essay, with the goal being to demonstrate how the multigenre version created spaces for me to contend with the silences in Connors's essay, my initial reading of it, as well as the multigenre form itself. I conclude with a revised response to Connors's essay, one informed by my new knowledge, which both critiques Connors's position as it affirms my investment in identifying with a feminist composition community from which I hesitate to separate myself. Specifically, I examine my resistance to recent feminist compositionists' calls for pedagogies that counter an "ethic of care" and advocate agonistic debate.

Chapter 5, "Teaching and Learning in Relational Spaces," continues this dual focus of theorizing multigenerity while problematizing feminist composition. Specifically, I explore how theories of performance and embodied delivery[3] can help feminist teachers disrupt the binaries of mother/bitch, ethic of care/agonistic debate within the classroom space. How might teacher subjectivity be theorized as a performance genre? How can feminist teachers migrate to different performance genres in order to disrupt students' expectations regarding what a feminist teacher is "supposed" to be? What discomforts do these migrations create for both teachers and students, and what can we learn from them? In response to these sorts of questions, I include reflections from me and three graduate students who joined me in a year-long journey to learn, practice, question, and revise feminist composition.

I conclude, I hope, by walking the talk. "On Lack, Progress, and Perfection" is a multigenre epilogue committed to exploring the usefulness of reconceiving of revision as progression toward wholeness rather than perfection.

Once, after explaining in some length my interest in multigenre texts to a more senior colleague, he said, "I hate texts that try to be cute." Stunned and angry, I shot back: "I don't think Gloria Anzaldúa would describe her work as 'cute.'" At the time, my colleague's comment angered me because it was so dismissive of my project; his saying it communicated to me that he had no desire to learn more about it. Furthermore, his use of the term "cute" to trivialize the scholarly and pedagogical value of multigenre texts (and, by extension, my project) reflected a sexist ideology that will forever spark my ire. Still, he (unintentionally) makes a point, one with which scholars of play are well acquainted: Anything that smacks of fun or pleasure is bound to be devalued in academic contexts, sites where rigor is synonymous with drudgery, and everything else is, well, cute.[4]

For those of us who believe in the revisionary potential of multigenre texts in particular, and in experimental texts in general, we need to anticipate dismissals like the one proffered by my colleague. In that specific situation, for example, I could have more effectively challenged my colleague's glibness by foregrounding the sociopolitical function of multigenre texts. In other words, if I had begun by theorizing the rhetorical effects of Anzaldúa's multigenre work, my colleague would have been unable to reject the value of such work so easily. This is to say, then, that we need to situate multigenre texts—the ones we write, read, and teach—within persuasive theoretical contexts. And while the student writing produced in response to multigenre assignments is often exciting and creative, we need something more complex than a show-and-tell of student work to persuade our colleagues to value multigenre scholarship and pedagogy. This book attempts to do just that.

Acknowledgments

Deep revision demands the presence of smart, committed readers; luckily I have had more than my fair share. Theresa Enos, Dana Fox, Thomas P. Miller, John Warnock, Tilly Warnock, Pat Youngdahl, Marvin Diogenes, Mary Beth Callie, Sandra D. Shattuck, Bob Broad, and my graduate student colleagues in the Rhetoric, Composition, and the Teaching of English program at the University of Arizona read and responded to early versions of this project with careful attention to my words and an uncompromising belief in my purpose. Later versions benefited enormously from responses prepared by reviewers Ginny Crisco, Juan Guerra, Marie Montaperto, Jason McIntosh, Richard E. Miller, and Nancy Welch. As my SWR editor, Robert Brooke encouraged this project by situating his suggestions for revision within a context that felt both professionally astute and pedagogically wise. I'm not sure why, but for some reason late in the revision process, I expected him to *tell* me what to do. Thankfully, he resisted this expectation, instead trusting me to figure out in consultation with others what I might change, how, and why. I am grateful, too, for the expertise of the editorial staff at Southern Illinois University Press who helped me bring this long journey to its end.

This project would not have been possible without the generosity of the male writing teachers who allowed me to interview them and who shared their feelings about teaching with such candor. I deeply appreciate the care and respect with which they treated my research, and I hope the knowledge I construct from those interviews is of use to them. The graduate students enrolled in my Feminist Composition and Rhetorics of Scholarship courses helped me think through many of the issues raised in this book, and I am grateful for their willingness to teach and learn alongside me. Marie Moeller, Teryn Robinson, and Zoé Younker, whose contributions appear in chapter 5, were especially helpful in encouraging me to rethink my attitudes toward and practice of feminist pedagogy. Additionally, I am grateful to the undergraduate students at Illinois State University who allowed me to study, cite, respond to, and learn from their writing.

My colleagues in the Writing Programs at Illinois State University have built a community where writing about teaching and teaching about writing are processes equally invigorating and robust. I feel fortunate to be working among them. As my chair, Ron Fortune was especially wonderful, encouraging me to make as many (dis)connections across my teaching and research as I could muster. I am also grateful for a summer grant from the Illinois State University College of Arts and Sciences, which made it possible for me to research and write portions of this book.

Mary Beth Callie, Christopher C. De Santis, Stacey Gottlieb, Kirstin Hotelling Zona, and Sandy Shattuck are friends and colleagues whose prodigious writing talents and unwavering loyalty motivate me to keep writing. Rob Isaacs—the surfing accountant, who embraces Burkean metaphor with such confidence and grace— nurtures me and my work with a generous spirit and a sharp mind. I am deeply grateful for his unquenchable curiosity about all things and his courageous willingness to live in revision with me.

Finally, though they don't always understand *what* I write, my family has always been supportive of my decision *to* write, and I thank them for reading with compassion my version of our shared past, as I know their versions would be different.

Revisionary Rhetoric, Feminist Pedagogy, and Multigenre Texts

1 / Writing That Listens
Defining Revisionary Rhetoric

My interest in exploring the revisionary potential of multigenre texts began several years after I started collecting semester portfolios. Although I had grown to appreciate the way portfolios allowed me to consider students' rough drafts, revision processes, and peer review commentary in the course of evaluating their course grades, I nevertheless started to have my doubts about that first portfolio text: the reflective letter. Specifically, I was troubled that so many of these letters seemed to follow the same narrative arc: the former writer—the unenlightened, perhaps even ignorant one—struggles mightily, and with the help of a great teacher and a few caring peers, is able in the span of sixteen weeks to realize some very important things about writing, learning, and life itself. Although many of these narratives made me feel good about myself and my teaching, with time I began to wonder if they were useful to my students. The letter's purpose, after all, was to help my students build metaknowledge of themselves as readers and writers. Did such simplistic narratives of progress really help them do that? I do not doubt that many of my students experienced some sort of genuine transformation as a result of their classroom experiences, but I also sensed their opening letters more accurately demonstrated their abilities to jump through hoops than their acquisition of useful reflective knowledge.

To encourage my students to resee their semester experiences in more complex ways, I toyed briefly with the idea of asking them to reflect on their weaknesses as writers and their negative experiences as students. I soon realized, however, that requiring them to do so in a genre so clearly designed to create a positive evaluative context would be problematic, if not unethical. Instead, I opted to make such reflection the subject of a separate essay, one students could omit from their final portfolios if they chose to do so. Because one of my major goals as a teacher is to help students forge connections across all their learning experiences, both in and out of school, I invited them to include texts written in classes across the curriculum as well as emails, journals, letters, and any other texts they felt related to their semester experience. Thus my first multigenre essay assignment was born.

As students gathered representative texts and started to juxtapose them, they became anxious and confused. "How are we supposed to make these connect?" they asked. I admitted that I was new to the assignment myself and that perhaps I could best help them by bringing in a rough draft of my own. Later that week, I shared my initial effort with my students—a rough assemblage of journal entries, excerpts from a mystery-in-progress, a conference presentation I had delivered earlier that term, a memo to my boss (the director of composition), and a poem. I explained that I did not yet understand how these texts were connected, but I felt they were all important. "I guess figuring out why is what I still need to do," I said. My students' review letters, which I had asked them to write in response to my draft, were sweetly complimentary, particularly in regards to my journal writing, but one student best represented their common critique when he wrote, "That thing was so damn confusing all I can do is ask questions." Almost all of my students wanted to know why I had included texts that were so different. They expressed delight in learning that I was trying to write a mystery, and they asked if I was writing it "for fun" or "for school." They wondered which kind of writing I like better—the "boring" conference paper type or the "honest" insights explored in my personal journal.

Looking back, I see how my students' reviews launched my interest in interpreting readerly confusion as something useful. Although I had been focused on finding the connections among my disparate texts, my students' confusions expressed in questions prompted me to redirect my attention to their generic differences. The students helped me recognize the potential of multigenre texts to construct complex and often contradictory identity formations. Furthermore, their confusion made it quite clear that juxtaposing genres within a single text disrupts readers and delays meaning making, and that such disruptions can result in reader responses that force writers to revise more deeply. In other words, none of my students wrote review letters that said, "It was good. I liked it." Nor did any of them offer me specific advice on ways to make my meaning more clear. Instead, as genuine collaborators in the process of revision, they encouraged me to listen hard to what I had not yet said.[1]

I offer this opening narrative to illustrate the usefulness of theorizing revision in terms that run directly counter to the way most of us practice it: as a process of *delaying* clarification of meaning so that differences can be heard, explored, and understood. Before continuing with my argument, however, I step back and situate this disruptive theory/practice of revision within a larger historical and scholarly context. My purpose in doing so is to demonstrate the ways in which current theories of knowledge making demand a revisioning of revision.

Revision: From Editing to Problem-Solving

Revision has not always been considered an important part of the writing process. In fact, as Jill Fitzgerald explains in an overview article on revision research, Aristotle made revision synonymous with error-correction or copyediting, and the view that revision is something that happens *after* a piece of writing is complete remained the norm until the late 1970s.[2] In her book-length study of revision, Fitzgerald continues that such an understanding of revision reflects positivistic beliefs about knowledge-making; that is, knowledge, which exists "out there," is arrived at by engaging in an objective and distanced process of discovery. According to this theory, writers revise by reading some external source, such as a style manual, in order to learn rules for identifying and correcting errors, which they then apply to their all-but-edited drafts. Revision studies prior to the 1970s confirm this understanding of revision and knowledge-making as researchers focused on final versions of texts produced by individual writers and tried to determine the specific textual features that made them "good." Their goal, we can assume, was to discover knowledge that could then be included in grammar work-books and style manuals.

In the late 1970s and 1980s, as composition researchers began to examine the composing processes of individual writers, theories describing revision as a complex, recursive process began to emerge. These theories departed from the traditional idea that revision was something done to a written product. Instead, researchers theorized revision as a process through which writers see their texts again and thereby create rather than correct their written products. According to Fitzgerald ("Research"), Donald Murray was a major contributor to this changing view of revision, as he was one of the first to theorize revision as an epistemological process that occurs within individual writers. In his landmark essay, "Internal Revision: A Process of Discovery," published in 1978, Murray defines writing as rewriting and distinguishes the polishing work of *external* revision—"what writers do to communicate what they have found written to another audience" (91)—from the knowledge-making process of *internal revision*—"everything writers do to discover and develop what they have to say, beginning with the reading of a completed first draft" (91). Whereas external revision involves making changes based on the needs and expectations of one's intended reader, Murray explains that during internal revision, the audience is the writer herself rereading her evolving text to discover meanings not yet made clear; positioned as her own best reader, the revising writer creates a space for her text to respond.

Donald Murray's theory suggesting two different kinds of revision, which are linked to particular kinds of reading (reading-to-make-clear vs. reading-to-discover), has been supported by empirical research conducted on the revision processes of individual writers. Exploring the question of how revision contributes to better writing, researchers in the later 1970s and throughout the 1980s conducted studies contrasting the revision processes of beginning writers with those of expert, or published, writers. The results of these studies parallel Murray's distinctions (see Armstrong; Bridwell; Faigley & Witte; Flower et al.; Matsuhashi & Gordon; Perl; Sommers). That is, novice writers limit their opportunities to discover

content because they assume their content already ₑ
writers, revision is about "fixing" errors, leading th
lexical rather than conceptual changes. They make rₑ
mous with copyediting, a skill that is best applied t
it is written.

According to Fitzgerald (*Towards*), these empirical revision studies, while generating useful information about the ways expert read-
ers/writers identify and solve problems, are insufficient because they
assume the existence of universal "truths" about what makes for good
writing, truths that can be discovered through observing experts'
processes and then taught to students writing in completely different situations. What is lacking in these studies, she contends, is a
theory of knowledge-making that foregrounds the social contexts
within which people must create meaning for themselves and others.

Revision as a Process of Convergence

Fitzgerald argues for the necessity of a rhetorical model for studying
revision, what she calls a Social-Interactive Model, one that focuses
on linkages between reader and writer. In such a model, the desired
knowledge is not universal and decontextualized rules and cognitive
solutions that lead to good writing but, rather, an awareness of how
people work together to construct a shared reality. Knowledge is
thought to be situation-dependent, with writers learning to write by
writing and thinking about writing in specific contexts. Fitzgerald's
epistemological model enables her to arrive at a necessarily social
definition of revision: "a process of social negotiation among participants in communities of writers and readers" (48). Using such a
model, the cognitive "problems" observed in the earlier empirical
studies are redefined as incongruities in writers'/readers' expectations.
According to Fitzgerald, while the empirical studies do discuss a
writer's need to consider her audience, these studies characterize such
needs in terms of a writer's static goal; that is, writers working in isolation decide how best to connect with their audience, and their failures to do so are described as "cognitive breakdowns" rather than as
miscommunications between writers and readers. Thus, the challenge

for writers during revision is not to apply generalizable cognitive solutions but rather to analyze the ways in which an audience's needs and expectations are defined by particular situations. Once such knowledge is determined, the writer can then revise to fill in knowledge gaps, to dissolve incongruities, and to achieve "reciprocity" and "a state of convergence" (40) with the reader.

This tendency to describe revision as a moment of convergence between writer and reader is discussed in a book that appeared eight years before Fitzgerald's. Titled, aptly enough, *Convergences: Transactions in Reading and Writing* (Petersen) and published by NCTE in 1986, the book contains essays by various scholars within the field, many of whom theorize revision as a convergence of both processes and people: writing and reading, author and audience. In "The Writing/Reading Relationship: Becoming One's Own Best Reader," for example, Richard Beach and JoAnne Liebman Kleine describe revision as a pivotal moment in the writing process when a writer must reread his text from the perspective of his intended reader. That is, he must *analyze* his audience in order to *become* his audience and thereby revise effectively.

So, we come full circle. In 1978, Donald Murray theorized revision as both a writer's internal process of learning what she wants to say as well as an external process of making that knowledge meaningful to someone other than herself. The empirical researchers conceptualized what that internal process might look like, and the rhetoricians reminded us that what is inside is tied to what is outside, and we're missing the big picture if we try to separate them. Despite these differences in theory and methodology, however, one common assumption remains: that timely convergence is a good thing.

Revision as a Process of Delayed *Convergence*

When we theorize revision as a process of dissolving incongruities between readers' and writers' expectations, we fail to ask a critical question ripe with social and political implications: *Why* do those incongruities exist in the first place? In other words, when the goal of revision is thought to be only achieved *consensus* in meaning, writers bridge gaps before they have time to discover them and explore why they might exist. Such a theory of revision reaffirms Catherine Lamb's point that "[a]s a culture, we learn much more about how to repress or ignore conflict than how to live with and transform it" (18); it also seems to work against the goals of teachers who promote cultural critique in their composition classrooms.[3] More specifically, in writing classrooms where students are expected to analyze a range of voices participating in debates about contemporary social issues, teachers need a theory of revision that motivates students to hear *a full range* of those voices. The revision models discussed above, however, which advocate consensus over difference, contradict the postmodern epistemologies on which such courses are typically founded.

In the following table, I summarize the above discussion in order to demonstrate how different theories of revision reflect certain epistemologies that in turn define the purposes of composition. In the first three theories of revision, the reader-writer relationship is theorized in terms of connections and consensus; in the fourth, which I have termed a rhetorical-cultural model, I begin to define a relational rhetoric that helps us read and contend with disconnections as well. In so doing, I seek to focus our attention on the ways in which delaying consensus might actually foster understanding among participants within communities where conflicts exist and where participants believe in the need to give voice to the differences that create them.

In *Getting Restless: Rethinking Revision in Writing Instruction*, Nancy Welch calls for a similar revision of the discipline's understanding of revision. Writing to scholars in composition studies who seek to understand revision as something more complex than a "stage" in a process model of composing, who seek to disrupt the notion that revision is simply about managing meaning, writing clearly, and reaching consensus, Welch argues that we must begin to theorize revision as an alchemic and necessarily social moment, both for the writer and in the writing. She draws on feminist psychoanalytic theory to venture a theory of revision that welcomes "dis-orientation" in the gaps between drafts. Such dis-orientation,

Revision Theory	Goal of Revision	Epistemology	Purpose of Composition	Revision Strategies
Stage Model				
Revision is defined as editing.	To produce technically correct texts that do not confuse or offend readers who expect flawless prose.	Positivistic. Knowledge is thought to reside within a text and a reader's job is to apprehend that meaning, to read "properly" and to uncover its single "true" meaning. Knowledge is revealed rather than made.	Students learn to write correctly.	Writers identify and fix surface feature errors as outlined in style manuals and grammar workbooks. Writers make lexical rather than conceptual changes to the existing text.
Problem-Solving Model				
Revision is a process whereby individual writers solve cognitive breakdowns in meaning-making by rereading their evolving texts in terms of their defined goals.	To solve communication problems that result in a writer's failure to achieve her defined goal of communicating her purpose to her target audience.	Knowledge is both revealed and made.	Students learn how to set goals and achieve them through the writing process.	Writers reread their texts often in order to identify problems and then draw on a repertoire of strategies to fix them. Writers consider both their purposes and the needs of their audience. Writers make both lexical and conceptual changes to the existing text.

she argues, enables writers to hear and contend with silences left unchecked in their previously "clear" versions. Welch's work elucidates many of my own concerns about the study of revision in our discipline, and my project, which locates revision within the dual contexts of feminist rhetoric and the multigenre essay form, seeks to answer some of her calls for further research.

Revision Theory	Goal of Revision	Epistemology	Purpose of Composition	Revision Strategies
Social-Interactive Model				
Revision is a process of negotiation among communities of writers and readers.	To construct a shared reality; to reach consensus, to achieve reciprocity or a state of convergence with one's reader; to be understood by one's reader.	Knowledge is situation-dependent and is constructed by participants in specific contexts.	Students learn how to analyze rhetorical situations.	Writers reread their texts often from the perspective of their intended audience. Writers remove or change passages that conflict with the expectations of the community. Writers make both lexical and conceptual changes to the existing text.
Rhetorical-Cultural Model				
Revision is a process of delaying consensus so that conflicts can be sustained, analyzed, and understood.	To understand the differences that exist between writers and readers; to explore the roots of disagreement.	Knowledge is situation-dependent and is constructed by participants in specific contexts.	Students learn how conflicts are constructed and mediated in and through language.	Writers reread their texts often looking for biased assumptions, contradictions, and potentially inflammatory passages. Writers write more about rather than eliminate passages that create conflict within the community. Writers make both lexical and conceptual changes to the existing text.

Defining Revisionary Rhetoric

Situated at the intersection of feminism and revision, I define revisionary rhetoric as a rhetoric of relationship, one grounded in a feminist postmodern epistemology that seeks to disrupt the binary logic inherited from the Enlightenment. In deconstructive terms, revisionary rhetors break down binaries in order to hear silences, to give active audience to the other side of the backslash. In Bakhtinian terms, revisionary rhetors demonstrate their commitment to hearing difference by privileging the centrifugal forces in a given discourse, those voices that disrupt the unifying tendencies of monologic thinking and writing. They strive to blur the supposed rigid boundaries that give rise to binaries such as public/private, content/form, reading/writing, and theory/practice. Consequently, as Rachel DuPlessis argues, a feminist-inspired rhetoric necessarily demands new forms of writing, for nothing changes through content alone. According to DuPlessis, such a rhetoric would focus on plurality, not mastery. That is, texts would be written in a way that works against universalizing tendencies. Instead, they would help readers realize that there are no unitary readings but only partial and multiple ones. Both DuPlessis and Diane Freedman explain the importance of the writer/reader relationship in a feminist-informed rhetoric. This relationship develops, continues Freedman, when texts seek to create intimacy between writer and reader rather than exercise power over one or the other.

In defining revisionary rhetoric, I affirm the work of feminist scholars who have come before me. In describing revisionary rhetoric as a rhetoric of *relationship,* I vigorously contest the disciplinary commonplace that relationship equals connection and understanding. Instead, I draw attention to the fact that all human relationships, including those that exist between readers and writers, enjoy moments of intimacy, closeness, and connection, but they also involve inevitable separation, loss, misunderstanding, disappointment, and pain. As I discussed earlier, theories and practices of revision within composition studies have focused on a writer's attempts to revise in order to reach consensus and connect with her audience. The assumption is that in order to be persuasive, writers should remove those textual moments that might offend or confuse potential readers. Of course, this assumption is well founded, especially for those of us who teach first-year composition and understand the frustrations of reading offensive and/or confusing writing. Yet, in privileging clarity and connection in our work on revision, I believe we have failed to theorize how readers and writers contend with the inevitable disconnections that permeate their experiences with texts. We can, of course, simply ignore that these moments exist; we can teach our students to delete them from their drafts all in the name of "effective" revision. But to do so, I think, would be to send a troubling message to our students: namely that when they cannot relate to or connect with something they read, they can simply skip it, ignore it, forget about it, and move on.

In this book, I explore some of the possible benefits of augmenting our understanding of revision by exploring its dark side: those spaces where readers and listeners, writers and speakers, fail to connect. I ask that we consider ways we might contend with these disconnections so that we might stop denying them and instead start learning from them. To help move us in that direction, I theorize a relational rhetoric that acknowledges the reality that people do not always want to hear what we have to say. Such a rhetoric is founded on the assumption that people are more willing to listen to us talk about a potentially painful subject if, in the telling, we indicate our own willingness to listen to them in return. However, as a patently *feminist* rhetoric, revisionary rhetoric as I define it must also acknowledge the reality that listening always takes place within contexts of asymmetrical power relationships. As such, listeners need not—nor should they—submit themselves to the onerous task of listening patiently to the discourses of those who seek to oppress them. Rather, listening in these situations (as I discuss in detail in chapter 4) emerges even more so as a process of interrogating oppressive assumptions that circulate among participants within specific discursive contexts.

Throughout this book, I examine specific textual practices that demonstrate a writer's willingness to listen with what Min-Zhan Lu describes as a "critically affirmative" ear ("Redefining," 173). Two of these practices, metadiscursivity and intertextuality, enable writers to acknowledge their texts as cultural constructions, thereby making themselves vulnerable by admitting up front the partial nature of their texts. Such practices create gaps, or silences, out of which readers can respond. I argue that it is this ability to respond that makes revision possible. I specifically analyze the ways in which multigenre texts foster readerly response, and I argue for more of them, both in the field and in the classroom, for they demand the kind of rereading that is necessary to practice a relational rhetoric. In short, I ask that rhetors seek to make themselves heard by demonstrating their commitment to listening to others; I ask that you join me in finding ways to write writing that listens.

Where Feminism and Revision Meet

In both feminist and composition studies, revision inspires hope, for it suggests that change is possible. Traditionally, academic feminists have viewed canonical revisions as forms of political action. By revising the word, we hope to change the world. Writing teachers also look to revision as a hopeful move, for students who reread and rewrite their texts often improve them. Consequently, feminist theories are especially useful in theorizing revision as a process of delaying consensus so that differences can be explored and understood.

Despite the obvious overlaps between feminist and revision studies, this research has only just begun, perhaps because feminism came to the discipline relatively late.[4] Whatever the reasons for its delay, feminism arrived definitively to composition studies in February 1995, when Elizabeth Flynn, in a *College English* article reviewing two book-length feminist projects, christened a new subfield: feminist composition. Scholars working in this subfield, she explains, draw on feminist scholarship in a variety of disciplines to extend "explorations of composition from a feminist perspective" ("Review," 201). In her naming and description of this new subfield, Flynn legitimizes the importance of feminist theories in composition studies and the need to critique these theories as we import them into a new disciplinary context. However, despite the growing popularity of feminist composition (see Phelps and Emig; Jarratt and Worsham), disciplinary overviews do not have much to say about feminist rhetorics. In *Fragments of Rationality,* for example, Lester Faigley summarizes research that explores connections between feminist theory and composition, but he says nothing about feminist *rhetoric* per se (35–37); in Ray Linn's *A Teacher's Introduction to Postmodernism,* feminist theory is folded into a chapter on multiculturalism, and there is no mention of feminist rhetoric.[5] Consequently, there are good reasons for intersecting feminism and revision and contending with the fallout, which is the goal of this book. The first, and most obvious, is to rethink revision as both a political ideology and a textual practice. The second is to contribute to a developing conversation about feminist rhetorics by gathering diverse disciplinary voices to define a feminist-inspired revisionary rhetoric of relationship.

In the remainder of this chapter, I introduce the following key terms, which I track throughout this book, terms that emerge at the intersection of feminism and revision and inform an understanding of revision as a process of delayed connection:

- Silence and Listening,
- Margins and Borders,
- Reading and Responsibility.

In selecting these terms, I emphasize the need for a revision theory that addresses contending with textual disconnections within a feminist context committed to building alliances across fields of difference. I also situate my theory within a growing body of scholarship interested in exploring the revisionary potential of listening to those perspectives that challenge readers' existing senses of self. As such, revisionary rhetoric is committed to listening to those voices which are too easily silenced and often reside on the margins/borders. Furthermore, it is a rhetoric concerned with the hard work of (re)reading in order to hear those perspectives that are easily ignored on first reading. Finally, revisionary rhetoric advocates writing in ways that facilitate rhetorical listening; it is a rhetoric that demands both to be heard and responded to; as such, it is a rhetoric that makes response possible.

Silence and Listening

In her review of Jennifer Luke and Carmen Gore's *Feminisms and Critical Pedagogies,* Gesa Kirsch examines how the fields of education and women's studies intersect to form feminist critical pedagogy, a subfield that, "like critical pedagogy, is concerned with questions of power, equity, and authority in the classroom, but it adds gender as a critical factor into the equation" ("Review," 723). Dissatisfied with male scholars' lack of attention to issues of gender, Luke and Gore gather essays grounded in critical pedagogy and postmodern discourse that collectively deconstruct popular terms such as voice, empowerment, dialogue, and collaboration. Kirsch concludes her review by arguing that silence is an important and undertheorized issue in feminist pedagogy, one that feminist scholars in rhetoric and composition studies must explore more thoroughly.

Intersecting revision and feminist theories is one way to hear Kirsch's call, as silence emerges in both contexts as a key term with positive and negative connotations. Donald Murray's (*Expecting*) description of revision as a process of listening for the unexpected surprise in evolving texts foregrounds listening as participatory silence, a necessary pause wherein texts speak back to writers and promote creative change. Murray encourages revising writers to reread for what they have not yet written, paying attention to the silences in their texts and allowing themselves to be surprised by the possibilities those silences afford. To be surprised by one's text, a writer needs to read with openness, receptivity, and a listening ear. It is this willingness to listen to the unplanned meaning in language that fosters an atmosphere of creative silence needed to revise well.

The belief in the artist's need for creative silence has been effectively problematized by feminist scholars, who argue that traditional representations of creative silence—the artist working alone in his garret, for example—undermine the social and political contexts within which art is produced and distributed. Thus, writers, such as Tillie Olsen, differentiate between "natural" silences—the artist's need for creative, reflective space, often denied to women—from "unnatural" ones, those voices silenced by the patriarchal practices of publishing and academic institutions. Olsen's book, aptly titled *Silences,* put the history of silence at the center of feminist theory. More recently, feminist poststructuralist theorists have examined silence within the context of discursive relationships, where silence can signify both presence and absence, oppressive gesture and empowering practice, thematic content and generic form.

In *Listening to Silences: New Essays in Feminist Criticism,* for example, editors Elaine Hedges and Shelley Fisher Fishkin gather essays that explore the often contradictory meanings assigned to silence in feminist contexts, thereby disrupting the belief that silence is "naturally good" or "bad." King-Kok Cheung's analysis of Joy Kogawa's novel, *Obasan,* for example, examines the function of what Cheung terms "attentive silence," a silence that results when readers are left with the task of piecing together parts of a text that do not make sense. More specifically, she analyzes how Kogawa's multivocal text, a text that is punctuated with silences, demands things from readers: "The reader must attend to the unarticulated linkages and piece together the broken parts; meaning permeates the spaces between what is said" (122). The reader is asked to "grasp an absent presence through imaginative empathy" (122), to feel what is not there and to begin to understand why.

This ability to fall silent in order to feel the absences in texts is especially important, contends Cheung, when readers are reading texts that do not reflect dominant cultural narratives. Kogawa's story in particular is about a young Japanese-Canadian woman's attempts to piece together the silences that thwart her own understanding of her family's history—the history of those family members who survived life in World War II internment camps as well as those who died in the bombings on Japan. Unable to call in familiar strategies for making sense of shared cultural stories, non-Japanese readers are made to fall silent as we struggle to understand the story's characters in ways Kogawa wishes them to be understood. Cheung's essay argues that reading for an understanding of cultural difference requires that readers be made to fall silent and engage in an attentive silence that helps us learn how to listen better.

This theme of the need for attentive silence in cross-cultural contexts is not limited to feminist literary theory. In *Saying and*

Silence, Frank Farmer turns to Bakhtin to explore the ways in which silences punctuate dialogic utterances. While discussing the concept of voice, for example, Farmer emphasizes the dialogic and therefore relational quality of voice (67). Implied in such an argument is the recognition that dialogue requires a silent, listening other. As such, Farmer's analysis dramatizes the degree to which *voice* frequently stands in for *dialogue,* thereby making invisible the dialogic function of listening. Farmer's book-length study is an attempt to locate firmly the listening Other in research on dialogue and silence, and it complements the work of other scholars who have turned a critical ear toward hearing listening as something more than the act of being silent.

In "When the First Voice You Hear Is Not Your Own," for example, Jacqueline Jones Royster argues that the construction of subjectivity is closely tied not only to how one speaks but also to how one is heard. To support her argument, she dramatizes three scenes, all of them occurring within professional contexts, that demonstrate how stereotypical listening limits the range of subjectivities available to minority people. For example, when she invokes an African American dialect while speaking, white audience members often compliment her for using her "authentic voice" in academic contexts. Such racist assumptions about what is "authentic" and what is not, she contends, prevent minority people from engaging in a wide range of voice constructions and ensures that those who choose to speak in "inauthentic" ways will not be heard. Her argument thus implicates the reader/listener in the construction of meaning and encourages us to find ways to promote respectful and honorable conversations across boundaries.

More recently, Krista Ratcliffe undertakes the challenge of defining something she terms rhetorical listening:

> To foreground listening in our field, I offer rhetorical listening as a trope for interpretive invention, one that emerges from a space within the *logos* where listeners may employ their agency—which Stanford drama theorist Alice Raynor defines as both 'capacity' and willingness (7)—to situate

themselves openly in relation to all kinds of discourse, whether written oral, or imagistic. (204)

Like Royster, Ratcliffe is interested in studying listening in such a way as to implicate the listener, to make her a responsible participant in the construction of the voices she chooses both to hear and ignore.

By focusing on a listener's agency, Royster, Ratcliffe, as well as Min-Zhan Lu ("Redefining"), demand that we consider the act of listening as something more than the "Yes, I hear what you're saying" response people like me too often produce in situations where we are supposedly committed to the project of dialogic understanding. While this Rogerian reflex helps to validate a speaker's existence, it is not an example of rhetorical listening. It does not allow the listener to own her reactions to the speaker's words; it does not obligate the listener to take responsibility for those reactions; nor does it force an examination of how those reactions are inextricably connected to the way she hears—and therefore sees—that speaker.

Before we get too comfortable, reminding ourselves that *surely* we respond in manners more complex than Rogerian validation (in fact, our scholarly research demands it), Ratcliffe outlines a few more types of "easy" response, those that prove we have listened but have yet to do so rhetorically. These include self-interested responses that range from "appropriation (employing a text for one's own end), to Burkean identification (smoothing over differences), to agreement (only affirming one's own view of reality)" (205). In each of these instances, we use or align ourselves with a speaker's words such that we ignore the *speaker's* reasons for saying them. Conversely, we also listen but ignore when we separate ourselves from the speaker through denial, guilt, and blame (204). These kinds of response create a relational distance between speaker/listener that makes forming alliances across differences impossible.

While I often encounter the above responses in the courses I teach, they do not appear so frequently in the scholarship I read. Instead, a more common type of easy response found in our professional scholarship is the defensively critical one. This is easy because it allows a listener to be critical of another without obligating her to consider the way she participates in the very thing she critiques. Personally, I know I'm on my way to this response when I throw the book (or journal) across the room. My stomach ties up in knots, and I imagine writing an email of the sort I have fortunately never sent. Simply put, I'm ANGRY. Someone has hit a nerve.

Rather than deny this emotional reaction, however, Ratcliffe and Lu encourage me to use it as a springboard for practicing rhetorical listening, demanding that I ask questions such as: Why am I so threatened by this speaker's argument? What is my personal/professional investment in defending that which this speaker challenges? In what ways are the speaker and I alike? In what ways are we different? How do these similarities and differences challenge my comfortable worldview? Indeed, in asking such questions, and exploring answers to them, I am on my way toward listening with a critically affirmative ear, one that enables me to use my initial reactions as points for revision (Lu, "Redefining," 176), as sites rich in their power to forge attitudinal change. Additionally, the emotional reaction I describe above illustrates how rhetorical listening can be, and perhaps should be, a disruptive process, one that forces listeners to account for themselves in ways that rock their comfort zones.

In sum then, together Royster, Ratcliffe, and Lu question the easy response, especially in situations for which differences in race, gender, sexual identity, class, age, body, etc. create huge experiential divides between speaker and listener. They imply that in these situations a lack of discomfort while listening makes dubious a person's desire to understand and learn from another. While most of us welcome the call for fluency in what Royster terms crossboundary discourse, these scholars argue that such fluency is possible only if the listener accepts her responsibility to hear in ways that might make her uncomfortable. As Ratcliffe explains:

> If such questioning [of ourselves, our attitudes and actions] makes us more uncomfortable, so be it. In fact, good. Such discomfort simply signifies already existing problems and underscores the need for standing under the discourses of ourselves and others—and listening. (210)

Before moving on, I want to make clear that I am not saying we should not be critical of each other's scholarship. To take such a position would be tantamount to embracing the easy responses of Burkean identification and agreement. Explaining how these too-close alignments eliminate the possibility of transformative dialogue, Farmer writes:

> [W]e should not seek to identify with the other, for to achieve such a condition would be to negate the possibility of a *relationship* with the other. Take away our mutual outsideness, and we will not mean anything to each other at all. (96, emphasis in the original)

Instead, the challenge, applying Lu's terminology, is to both critique the positions of others as we simultaneously affirm our own investment in those very positions. To accomplish this, Ratcliffe advocates a listening that "proceed[s] from within a *responsibility* logic," a "performance" that "locate[s] identification in the discursive spaces of both *commonalities* and *differences*" (204, emphasis in the original).

Margins and Borders

A second cluster of key terms that emerges at the intersection of revision and feminism is margins/borders. We write in the margins of our students' drafts, asking questions and demanding further inquiry. We write in the margins of the books we read, taking note of what we can use, what we are intrigued by, what we cannot understand. In both these roles, as writing teacher and academic reader, we intentionally interrupt one process (reading) with another (writing). In both, the margins represent spaces of creative interruption, the stopping of one process so that another might begin.

Similarly, in feminist contexts, "feminists have used a metaphor of marginality, of bringing women's voices from margins to the center and of standing on the margin, to reread the core of Western epistemology and rhetoric" (Ritchie and Ronald, 219). This rereading facilitates a theorizing of margins as sites for creative interruption, spaces where traditions and conventions are in flux and ill-defined and thus open to change. In *Composing a Life,* for example, Mary Catherine Bateson examines the lives of five women who, in different ways, experienced life interruptions that, while painful, caused them to grow in important ways. Bateson argues that these women have, over the course of their lives, developed a revising attitude that enables them to survive and learn from unwanted, unexpected interruptions. As such, Bateson theorizes revision as a life skill and an improvisatory art, one where people "combine familiar and unfamiliar components in response to new situations" (3). By reading about the lives of these women, who, more so than men, have learned how to respond to interruptions in a healthy fashion, Bateson argues that we can develop strategies for developing an openness to alternatives.

Another example of a feminist study dedicated to examining how work in the margins gives rise to creative change is Susan R. Van Dyne's *Revising Life: Sylvia Plath's Ariel Poems.* Van Dyne's book models a brand of revision studies where personal, theoretical, and textual contexts overlap and demonstrate how a writer's motivations to revise are culturally produced. More specifically, Van Dyne interprets twenty-five of Sylvia Plath's *Ariel* poems through three different but connected contexts: Plath's journal entries from 1957 to 1959, feminist theories, and Plath's multiple drafts of her poems. As Van Dyne argues in the opening sentence of her book:

> For Sylvia Plath, revising her life was a recurrent personal
> and poetic necessity. In her letters and journals as much as
> in her fiction and poetry, Plath's habits of self-representa-
> tion suggest she regarded her life as if it were a text that
> she could invent and rewrite. (1)

Van Dyne's central concern is to capture Plath's subjectivity in process; that is, by analyzing the contradictions that emerge when these three contexts intersect, Van Dyne is able to explore the contradictions among Plath's identities as middle-class wife, mother, and aspiring poet in 1950s America. As Van Dyne explains:

I locate agency in the female subject not only in the self-conscious performances of these texts but also in Plath's writing of a revisionary history. In her journals we see her as a discerning subject, interpreting her position in her culture. In the poems we see her refiguring the textual representation of that position and in the process rearticulating a changed female subjectivity. Finally, by revision I mean to suggest that ways that Plath repeatedly invested in, dismantled, and reconstructed the personae she performed in her life, in her letters and journals, and in these poems. (7)

In her extensive analyses of Plath's revisions, Van Dyne pays particular attention to their materiality. For example, she analyzes how Plath used the backsides of manuscripts written by her then husband, poet Ted Hughes, to draft her own writing:

Plath read and reread the reverse of these pages while composing, especially to get started or whenever she was stuck. The subversive revenge plots embedded in these poems become fully meaningful only when we read them in the context of his manuscripts that inspired and infuriated her. (34)

Angered by the female subjectivities she often found inscribed in Hughes's writing, Plath turned the sheet over and revised. Plath also drafted poems on pink Smith College letterhead, which she obtained while working there, but she turned the header upside down before writing (Van Dyne, 8, 53). Using these marginal spaces—the backside, the upside down—as sites of creative resistance, Plath models reinscription as a strategy for revision.

This theme of revision as the possibility for creative change comes up again and again in both feminist and composition contexts. Scholars in both disciplines often read the margins as places where creativity blossoms. Indeed, disciplines like rhetoric and women's studies herald their interdisciplinary nature, and scholars in both fields argue that working across different disciplines creates spaces where useful, revisionary knowledge can be imagined beyond the limits of traditional disciplinary conventions. Linking the importance of interdisciplinary work to feminist demands for social change, Mary Catherine Bateson argues that the "most creative thinking occurs *at the meeting places* of disciplines. . . . At the edges, where lines are blurred, it is easier to imagine that the world might be different" (73, emphasis added).

But if marginal spaces are sites for creative change, feminist scholars also remind us that because those working in them are marginalized, these sites can also be oppressive. In "Sideshadowing Teacher Response," for example, Nancy Welch problematizes the idea that teacher commentary in the margins of students' drafts is the best way to encourage revision. Arguing that no matter how "open-ended" and "non-directive" her responses might be, Welch explains that her comments nevertheless "take on weight and permanency" (376) and "work toward defining a reality" (376) for her students when, in fact, many realities are present. To work toward positioning the teacher's voice as one among many, Welch describes how students can be taught strategies for rereading and commenting in the margins of their *own* drafts.

A more dramatic example of the oppressive potential of marginal spaces is Gloria Anzaldúa's metaphor of the borderlands, which has become popular among rhetoric and composition scholars who strive to represent the interdisciplinary nature of their work.[6] But in her own use of the metaphor, Anzaldúa is careful to balance creative possibility with the reality of violence. In her study of cross-genre women's writing, including Anzaldúa's *Borderlands,* Diane Freedman connects oppression to creative expression by exploring how ethnic women writers cross genres and languages in their texts. More specifically, she explores how these women writers create textual borders that parallel the geographical, sexual, and social borders of their lives. As Freedman speculates:

> Perhaps the more marginalized one feels, the more one wants to blur the division between public and private life and language and to resist both dualism and separatism by

crossing from language to language, genre to genre, discipline to discipline, writer to reader. (71)

Thus, these writers use creative textual practices to battle against the oppressive consequences of dualistic, separatist thinking.[7]

Similarly, in Van Dyne's analysis of Plath's revising process, we see another example of how the marginal space can be both creative and oppressive. In what she calls Plath's "one last attempt at balance" (170), Van Dyne recounts Plath's final days before committing suicide in February 1963. In an effort to remake her life in the wake of her divorce from Hughes, Plath moved to London and took up residence in Yeats's former home, a move that she hoped would help her return to her writing. At this time Plath was, as Van Dyne observes, a woman whose husband had left her, a mother attempting to raise two children alone, and a daughter/writer trying to change the family narrative she most wanted to revise—to not be like her own mother. Despite her hopefulness, Plath was never able to devote herself to her writing as she planned. Within days London was immobilized by one of the biggest winter storms in its history. Alone and depressed in a drafty flat with a nonworking phone, Plath was unable to hire a nanny to help with child-rearing; thus, she found little time to write. On the back of a draft of Plath's poem "Kindness" are two lists for possible "mother's helpers," none of whom was ever hired (Van Dyne, 170). Three times Plath tried to muster the energy to leave her home and venture out into the snow to buy diapers for her children, and three times she failed. In "Kindness," Plath writes that "the blood jet is poetry." Van Dyne argues that in drafting this poem, Plath tried to rewrite women's productive legacy, to find a way for women to create and live on through their writing rather than by having children. Yet, as Van Dyne observes, the back of the poem's draft, with its list of mother's helpers, reveals Plath's culturally and materially gendered contradictory position (170). Taken together, the poem and the list demonstrate the duality of marginal work: On the one hand there is the hope that things can be different; on the other is the reality that hope is never enough.

(Re)reading and Responsibility

A final cluster of key terms that emerges at the intersection of revision and feminism is rereading and responsibility. Of course, in composition contexts, rereading is understood to be a necessary component in the revision process, as writers must reread their texts in order to write again. Similarly, in feminist contexts, rereading has been a primary way of rethinking canonical texts and the traditions that create them. Because rereading in so important in both fields, scholars in each have focused their efforts on rereading reading. In their introduction to *Gender and Reading,* for example, Elizabeth Flynn and Patrocinio P. Schweickart consider the implications of the term "responsibility" in masculinist vs. feminist contexts. Citing Carol Gilligan's work, the authors explain that in the former context, responsibility is often associated with liability—one acts responsibly when he exercises his rights without infringing on those of others. In feminist contexts, however, responsibility is more closely tied to responsiveness to others' needs (xx), to ways of "minimizing pain and preserving relationships" (xx). This difference in meaning is reflected in Michael Hassett's essay, in which he describes the kinds of texts that enhance a reader's ability to respond, that is, a reader's response-*ability*.

One of my favorite essays that models this kind of feminist reading is Nancy Mairs's "In Search of 'In Search of Our Mothers' Gardens': Alice Walker." I've heard Mairs read aloud on several occasions, and always I marvel at the depths to which she is willing to go among strangers. She writes and talks candidly about her depressions, attempted suicide, adultery, MS. Reading Mairs reading Walker, I see how the first found her connection to the second and how I find my way to both of them. In her essay, Mairs redefines literary analysis by framing her close textual reading of Walker's essay within an autobiographical context. More specifically, Mairs locates her analysis within metadiscursive commentary that acknowledges her own anxiety about being a white, middle-class, academic "doing" Alice Walker. By recognizing her limitations as a reader, Mairs creates an expansive space that deepens her understanding of the text, its author, and herself. As such, Mairs's essay models how a feminist reading process transformed into written product functions *as* feminist rhetoric.

Mairs begins her essay with metadiscursive commentary that acknowledges her struggle to read and write as she knows she must:

> The process of writing in order to pull together the ideas that my reading has yielded remains essential to my construction of the world. It's about the hardest work I know, however, and so left to my own devices I'm apt to work double-crostics or call around town getting estimates on upholstery cleaning instead. (630)

Through an autobiographical lens, Mairs describes the context within which she approached the essay she is about to analyze: she was taking a class, she was trying to learn to write academically *and* personally, she was lonely, she was overeager in her attempts to shine as the class feminist. By revealing her struggles as reader and student, Mairs develops a feminist ethos founded not on mastery but on something else—a willingness to go *in search of*. This search begins when Mairs recognizes her own limitations. For examples, as she prepares for her class presentation on Walker, Mairs explains what she could not possibly do:

> I plunged almost instantly into despair. I had two weeks to prepare. I sensed before finishing the first essay that to do the right sort of job, I needed to read all of Alice Walker, as well as the work of Margaret Walker, Toni Morrison, Audre Lorde, Ann Allen Shockley, Toni Cade Bambara, Michele Wallace, and any number of other writers all the way back to Phyllis Wheatley and especially Zora Neale Hurston, together with everything I could lay my hands on in black feminist theory. (631)

And what she could not possibly be: "I was—and am—intractably white and thus, possibly by my very nature, incapable of accurately reading a black writer" (631).

But Mairs's essay does not end with this line, so as readers we understand that somehow Mairs finds a way "to do the right sort of job," and she does so, she tells us, by surrendering New Critical attachments and instead letting "Alice Walker teach me how to read Alice Walker" (632). With this move, Mairs illustrates how revisionary rhetors can learn to respond to texts they fear they cannot understand: They relinquish claims to mastery; by doing so they fall into despair; by falling into despair they become ready to listen.

Mairs's specific enactment of revisionary rhetoric takes on the form of a textual mirror: she reads Walker's essay by identifying key discursive strategies and then responds using those same strategies in her own essay. This mirroring process gives Mairs a way to read Walker and thereby overcome her initial despair, which ultimately brings her own response into being. The key strategy that Mairs both identifies as reader and uses as writer is that of inclusive revisioning of terms, concepts, and forms. Such revisions are undertaken by both authors so that old versions are stripped of their power to exclude. As Mairs explains, Walker invents new strategies, "both structural and symbolic, which disrupt the pattern of expectations imposed by the dominant literary tradition . . . so that what has not been permitted to exist can come into being" (632). For Walker, this means redefining what counts as art, who counts as artist. For Mairs, this means redefining what counts as "appropriate" literary analysis. Both rhetors redefine an exclusive tradition by

> employ[ing] and thereby validat[ing] many of the cognitive modes—indirection, associative reasoning, anecdotal development, reliance on folk wisdom and intuition—which patriarchal critics have traditionally devalued by ascribing them to women and other primitive thinkers. (632)

Mairs explains, for example, how the structural form of Walker's essay—with its unidentifiable thesis statement and its fifty (often one-sentence) paragraphs within the span of twelve pages—challenges composition pedagogies that stress conventional notions of "focus" and "development." Walker also revises actual text from

Virginia Woolf's *A Room of One's Own,* inserting "the realities of the black woman's history, broadening Woolf's view to encompass experiences of which Woolf would never have been aware" (633). On the sentence level, Mairs examines how Walker's breaks with syntactic convention create a sense of urgency, a feeling of movement. By "playing against convention" in both her content and structural form, Walker is able "to keep the reader unfixed, unlulled, open to [her] search" (633).

And it is by being open to Walker's search that Mairs eventually feels invited to join it. Following Walker's lead, Mairs contributes to the disruptive project by refusing to separate personal writing and literary criticism. Even her choice of title, which links Walker's essay to Walker the essay*ist,* acknowledges that an ethical quest to understand a writer's words must also include an attempt to understand the writer's relationship to those words. For Mairs, this ethical responsibility becomes both more challenging and necessary when the reader, by virtue of race, gender, class or sexual identity, feels removed from the text and anxious about reading it well. However, rather than disassociate herself from the text and its author with cop-outs like "I can't relate to this" or "It's not my job to interpret this," Mairs reads her anxiousness as a first step toward fuller listening, and she is able to "read" this anxiousness and feel its implications because she breaks generic form and actually *writes* it. Like Walker, who speaks the unspeakable by insisting on talking about spirituality and vaginas, topics that make most academic readers queasy and uncomfortable, Mairs also speaks the unspeakable, for she begins an academic literary analysis with a gesture that calls into question the ways we teach our students to build a credible ethos. However, viewed through the lens of revisionary rhetoric, Mairs's strategy works well. By writing about her struggles to read, Mairs creates, paradoxically, the very space within which she finds she can read well—she both hears Walker's words and responds with her own. Ultimately, it is by her initial acknowledgment of her own "writerly pickle" that Mairs becomes a more response-able reader.

Viewed through the lens of revisionary rhetoric, then, strategies for writing and reading are the same, and given our commitment to disrupting binaries, that is as it should be. By engaging in rigorous self-reflection while reading and writing, thinkers become revisers connecting with other revisers and themselves. They respond to texts in ways that invite those texts' authors to respond in turn. Through an ongoing process of acknowledging their partial worldviews, by making themselves vulnerable through their revelation of limitation, revisionary rhetors embrace disconnection; in doing so, they open the door to increased intimacy and understanding.

Even so, as anyone who has ever been in a significant relationship knows, disconnecting from others so that we might grow closer to them is a risky business. For the revisionary rhetor, the risks of delayed convergence—the discomfort of uncertainty, the fear of being misunderstood, the thwarted desire to belong—are real and the rewards not always so clear. My goal in the following chapters is to persuade you to believe the risks are worth taking.

2 / Do I Belong "in" RhetComp?

Revision, Identity, and Multigenre Texts

In "Reading and Writing the Family," Daphne Desser analyzes her responses to letters written by her great-grandfather, "a Russian Zionist and writer who lived as a Jewish person during a time of severe Russian persecution of ethnic difference" (314). After undertaking the laborious task of translating these letters, written (mostly in French) between 1924 and 27, Desser examines the process by which she identified with and disconnected from the ethos of the man constructed in translation. Although Desser's conclusion is an optimistic one—that the fluidity and contingency of ethos and identification make revision and renegotiation between self and other possible—her article makes clear that the process of identity (re)formation is not necessarily easy or pleasurable. In fact, Desser's analyses of translated passages that left her "shocked and dismayed," "baffled, confused and uncertain of how to interpret" (321)—passages where her great-grandfather surfaced as a man she did not like—dramatize the pain of translation, the slow, unfolding manifestation of disconnection.

In this chapter, I analyze the multigenre essay form *as* a rhetorical strategy, one that can be used to force the kind of dis-identification Desser describes above. Specifically, after defining and arguing for the place of multigenre texts in English studies, I analyze two such texts written by scholars in rhetoric and composition studies. Both authors—Nancy Welch and Richard E. Miller, respectively—juxtapose genres considered within and outside the purview of RhetComp, thereby causing readers who reside comfortably within the discipline's boundaries to dis-identify with the texts and its authors. From a revisionary rhetor's position, this initial dis-identification is the delay necessary to both challenge a dominant disciplinary identity and to create room for fuller, more complex definitions of what it means to be "in" RhetComp. First, however, I begin by outlining two textual strategies key to the practice of revisionary rhetoric—metadiscursivity and intertextuality. While these strategies can obviously be deployed in texts other than the multigenre essay, their revisionary potential can be more fully realized in the multigenre form, which demands new and better kinds of listening.

On the Limitations of Heteroglossia

Revisionary rhetors demonstrate their commitment to relationship by using two interrelated textual strategies: metadiscursive commentary and intertextuality. Together these two rhetorical strategies enable rhetors to give form to paradox as their writing both makes itself heard as it listens. In fact, I would push the envelope and say these rhetors make themselves heard precisely *because* they listen. The first textual strategy—the inclusion of metadiscursive commentary—helps collapse the writer/reader binary and works toward rebuilding relationship by authorizing both the writer and the reader. Through metadiscursive commentary, a writer's authority is built on something other than a mastery that screams: HERE'S THE WAY IT REALLY IS! Instead, a revisionary rhetor writing in a postmodern era relies on the belief that knowledge is always partial, even contradictory. As such, she realizes that the most useful way of developing her authority is to acknowledge that belief and build it into her writing through a self-reflective consideration of her own knowledge-making. As Nancy Mairs puts it: "As far as I'm concerned, my text is flawed not when it is ambiguous or even contradictory, but only when it leaves you no room for stories of your own" (*Voice*, 74). Metadiscursivity helps create this room by allowing the seams to show (Freedman, 25). By marking their texts as partial versions of some unknowable and revisable whole, revisionary rhetors create gaps that invite readers to speak back.

Intertexuality, which coincides with metadiscursivity, is a second strategy used by revisionary rhetors: As the metadiscursive moment reaches toward another voice, another view, the intertextual moment reaches back, filling in gaps with new and different versions that both work against and support the central text. In *The Disobedient Writer: Women and Narrative Tradition,* Nancy A. Walker argues that intertextuality in women's fiction and autobiography is a revisionary strategy because it enables authors to juxtapose texts in ways that challenge the legitimacy of dominant "truths." As Walker explains:

> To the extent that a narrative is referential to a prior narrative in its own construction, it calls attention to its own fictive and conditional character. Put another way, it becomes *a* narrative rather than *the* narrative, a construct to be set alongside other constructs. Thus this revisionary kind of narrative is closely allied to metafiction. Whereas metafiction calls attention to the conventions of creating fiction—its mechanisms of plot, character, and voice—the narratives I am addressing accomplish a similar end by calling attention to the elements of another version of the story. (6–7, emphasis in original)

One example of such an intertextual narrative that Walker analyzes in detail is Margaret Atwood's *The Handmaid's Tale,* a feminist revision of *The Scarlet Letter.* Specifically, Walker analyzes how Atwood revises on two levels. First, by telling her tale through a previously marginalized character's point-of-view, namely, Offred's, Atwood writes what Walker calls a "disobedient narrative," a narrative that "expose[s] or upset[s] the paradigms of authority inherent in the [text it] appropriate[s]" (7). This first level of intertextuality, which references a prior text—*The Scarlet Letter*—invites readers to question the "truth" of the tale presented by Hawthorne. Second, by situating Offred's version as one among many, by juxtaposing it with other kinds of contingent texts, including historical and biblical narrative and personal memoir, Atwood demands that the reader also "question the stability of Offred's tale. The fact that Offred narrates her story *as* a story that she constantly reminds us is a 'reconstruction' is an invitation to the reader to perform additional reconstructions" (155, emphasis in original). Thus, both outside and within her narrative, Atwood gathers texts in ways that demonstrate the contingency and constructedness of language and experience, thereby making the reader question the stability of text-as-truth. Rather than fill in "truths" for her readers, Atwood leaves them asking questions and performing additional reconstructions of their own.

In rhetoric and composition studies, one popular strategy for promoting intertextuality is to produce heteroglossic texts, those that literally include the voices of many different speakers. However, as Constance Coiner argues, simply including many voices in a single text does not ensure revisionary rhetoric. Specifically, she warns that the inclusion of many, disconnected voices is dangerous because the democratizing effect of heteroglossia is lost; there is only white noise, with everyone speaking but no one being heard. This "white noise" effect is dramatized in Lester Faigley's transcripts from his networked classroom (*Fragments*). As we know, Faigley has argued that the technology challenges teacher-centered authority and increases students' willingness to discuss previously "silenced" issues, thereby promoting heteroglossic texts that foreground unassimilated difference. However, as I read and reread those transcripts, I feel as if everyone is talking at once and no one is listening. The texts produced by Faigley and his students illustrate my point about the need for a rhetoric that moves beyond heteroglossia. Absent a writer's metadiscursive commentary, there is no room for intertextuality—there are simply the voices of the many scrambling to be heard but feeling no responsibility to listen.

Analyzing the problems and potentialities of student-generated hypertexts, Joseph Janangelo echoes my call for a writer's inclusion of critical commentary that helps readers "stimulate important connections" (30). Such commentary works against the white noise effect experienced in Faigley's networked classroom because it offers a "shaping strategy," a "specific poetics of collage" (27), that foregrounds the writer's rhetorical intentions. Rather than simply juxtaposing texts and hoping that readers have the patience and know-how to make useful linkages, Janangelo argues for a combination of metadiscursive commentary and minimalist background information that, when read with and against the primary text, generates a kind of open-ended, revisionary knowledge not accessible through more linear texts.

The challenge for revisionary rhetors, then, is to produce heteroglossic discourse that both listens well as it makes itself heard. Working in tandem, the textual features of metadiscursivity and intertextuality enable writers to meet this challenge by creating texts that contain gaps, which, when filled in by others, make room for fuller and deeper listening. In this way, revision becomes a process of consciously constructing gaps out of which I, you, we can respond.

Revisionary Rhetoric and Multigenre Texts

I define multigenre texts as experimental scholarly essays that are marked by the conscious juxtaposition of academic essay with other genres, including poetry, fiction, creative nonfiction, and drama. Multigenre texts differ from Clifford Geertz's "blurred genres," which have gained considerable popularity in the discipline (e.g., scholarly essays that blur autobiography, teaching narratives, and rhetorical theory). Unlike blurred genres, multigenre texts contain breaks—signified by white space on the printed page—that separate one genre from the next. I theorize multigenre texts as one type of multivocal discourse where the inclusion of diverse genres adds another layer of "vocality." Thus, an analysis of textual meaning can include the ways in which genre shapes a writer's subjectivity and how a writer's decision to include different genres within a single text enhances the possibility for metadiscursive, intertextual moments. Multigenre texts both enact a revisionary rhetoric and demonstrate ways writers can sustain revision by situating meaning within layered and multiple contexts. By disrupting an academic reader's genre expectations, these texts slow the reader down as she struggles to make meaning across a field of generic differences. In so doing, they create a revisionary space that highlights rather than silences cultural and ideological differences.

Multigenre texts are particularly useful in promoting revisionary rhetoric in academic contexts, which are full of good readers who are in the habit of reading quickly and well. Since one goal of revisionary rhetoric is to attend to silences, the writerly task of prompting better listening in academic situations must necessarily be a disruptive one. That is, when addressing privileged readers who are confident they can read well and thereby understand diverse points of view, revisionary rhetors seek to disrupt their readers' harmonious reading experiences by using textual strategies that delay immediate convergence of meaning. One such strategy is to compose multigenre texts, which prevent traditionally coherent readings because their juxtaposed genres eschew linear transitions. By encountering texts that are not obviously whole and unified, readers are asked to confront their confusions by reading more fully and contextually.

In a study of postmodern poetry, Jane Miller argues that the presence of textual ruptures implicates the reader in the making of meaning. By advocating initial discomfort that is alleviated by a reader's fuller, more contextual awareness, Miller contends that textual ruptures build relationship between writer and reader. The reader no longer consumes but instead participates. By providing these sorts of textual disruptions, multigenre texts promote better listening because they break down a reader/writer binary that positions the writer as a disembodied disseminator of "truth" and the reader as passive recipient. These texts instead create a participatory *relationship* between writer and reader, a relationship that holds both parties responsible for the construction of meaning.

One of the more frequently cited multigenre texts in rhetoric and composition studies is Gloria Anzaldúa's *Borderlands/La Frontera*. Like Pratt's "contact zone," Anzaldúa's "borderland" is popular in the discipline because it has been useful in foregrounding the politics of teaching and classroom interactions. For example, many scholars adopt the metaphor of "borderland" when describing the experiences of marginalized students encountering and confronting the conventions of university culture and, more specifically, academic writing.[1] For my purposes, Anzaldúa's text is important because it demonstrates how a multigenre text enacts revisionary rhetoric. In addition to juxtaposing memoir, poetry, and academic essay, Anzaldúa's text disrupts a traditionally coherent reading because it is written in multiple genres and languages. For example, in a chapter titled "How to Tame a Wild Tongue," Anzaldúa argues that to suppress a person's identity as it is constructed through language—that is, to refuse to allow someone to use all the languages that create her—is to make that someone ashamed of being herself. In a double move typical of revisionary rhetoric, Anzaldúa presents this argument as she claims her right to make it as she sees fit. Thus, we as readers encounter a chapter that opens with personal memoir written in English and moves quickly to cultural historical analysis written in both English and Spanish. Near the end of her chapter, Anzaldúa writes:

> [T]he struggle of identities continues, the struggle of borders is our reality still. One day the inner struggle will cease and a true integration will take place. In the meantime, *tenémos que hacer la lucha. ¿Quién está protegiendo los ranchos de mi gente? ¿Quién está tratando de cerrar la fisura entre la india y el blanco en nuestra sangre? El Chicano, si, el Chicano que anda como un ladrón en su propia casa.* (63)

As Donna Qualley explains:

> Anzaldúa's mix of poetry and prose, Spanish and English, and personal, mythic, and historical content pose a challenge for readers on this side of the border. Only as readers begin to grasp the dynamic and plural nature of the other—La Mestiza—do they begin to make sense of the text, and their own ways of reading (and being in the world) are disclosed and held open for inspection. (104)

Similarly, Diane Freedman explains that a privileged reader who cannot read Spanish encounters writing like the above and feels the experience of facing borders she cannot cross. The foreign language confuses her; its presence delays the progression of her reading. It is this confusion, this delay, that creates a space for the reader to hear more fully. If the reader is patient enough and is willing to listen to the silence of her own confusion, what she will hear, argues Kate Adams, is "some of the suppressed cultural history of the Mexican and Indian peoples of the Southwest that is prerequisite to our appreciation and understanding of her Northamerican experience" (135). Anzaldúa's text thus breaks "long silences, countering the lies of racist and ethnocentric history with creative speech" (Adams, 137) and gives voice to the painful experiences of a lesbian of color living in a variety of conflicting borderlands. Anzaldúa's multigenre text, as a social act, bears witness to a legacy of silence and oppression; it demands "a wider, deeper listening" (Adams, 140); it leads "us to the kind of silence that is prerequisite to our hearing new and vital voices on their own terms" (Adams, 141).

Anzaldúa's text thus achieves another goal of revisionary rhetoric: namely, it breaks down a form/content binary by folding the two sides in on themselves. For Anzaldúa, the form *is* the content and vice versa. By offering up her text as a borderland, one in which the reader struggles to survive as a meaning-maker, Anzaldúa promotes an experiential sharing between writer and reader, a sharing that works against disembodied and dispassionate readings. Instead of simply telling her story and arguing for creative dissonance, Anzaldúa writes in such a way as to make us feel her story with her. We are prevented from simply nodding our heads in that common scholarly manner, "Hmmm, yes. Very interesting." Instead, we feel uncomfortable. "What is she doing?" we ask. Maybe we feel angry: "I can't read this! How am I supposed to make sense of it?" In short, we not only read about her life, we are also made to feel something in response to her writing of her life, and we move (I hope) from confused emotion to empathic listening to fuller understanding.

Disrupting English Subjects: Revising Identity in RhetComp and Beyond

To help move us in this direction, Jacqueline Jones Royster argues that we must become more fluent in what she terms "cross-boundary discourse," a discourse where speakers' subjectivities shift and blur, and that to acquire this fluency we must learn new strategies for speaking and listening. Within English studies departments, where the subjects of literature, creative writing, rhetoric and composition, and linguistics are *supposed to* blur and where the subjectivities of those who teach in these areas could use *more* blurring (see Bishop, Malinowitz), multigenre texts have enormous potential. More specifically, because multigenre texts are by definition a composite of diverse genres and identities, they can potentially expose and thereby force us to contend with the silenced tensions that exist within most English studies departments. In his description of a "fusion-based" curriculum, for example, Stephen North describes the mixed genre assignments his graduate students produced, texts that enabled them to make (dis)connections among the various fields within English and thereby take advantage of the friction that exists (73).

Arguing more generally about the disciplinary benefits of genre study, both Amy J. Devitt and Anis Bawarshi view rhetorical genre analysis as a conduit to increased communication among the disparate fields that compose English studies. Cognizant of the power dynamics that deter effective collaboration between literature and composition, Devitt nevertheless posits that the diverse emphases of the two fields

> can be encompassed within a genre theory that sees genres as involving readers, writers, texts, and contexts; that sees all writers and readers as both unique and as necessarily casting themselves into common, social roles; that sees genres as requiring both conformity with and variation from expectations; and that sees genres as always unstable, always multiple, always emerging. (715)

Similarly, Bawarshi theorizes genre in such a way as to

> allow us in English Studies to expand and synthesize our field of inquiry to include the constitution of all discourses and the identities implicated within them, thereby helping us to rethink our at times unhealthy distinctions between

> literary and nonliterary texts, poetics and rhetoric, author
> and writer, literature and composition, and focus instead
> on how all texts, writers, and readers are constituted by the
> genres within which they function. (358)

By making visible the (dis)connections that exist among those who teach and research within English departments, multigenre texts can be analyzed to augment our understanding of the rhetorics of English studies, thereby helping us make more persuasive arguments about the importance of rhetoric and composition(ists) within them. Furthermore, by analyzing such texts written by people who already identify as members of a RhetComp community, we can question and revise the commonplaces of our home discipline as we move within and outside it. To these ends, I offer the following analyses of two multigenre texts—Nancy Welch's "Toward an Excess-ive Theory of Revision" and Richard E. Miller's "The Nervous System."

In her book-length study of revision, *Getting Restless: Rethinking Revision in Writing Studies,* Nancy Welch argues against theories of revision that view it as a "one way movement from writer-based to reader-based prose" (137), pedagogies that ask revisers to do away with "passages that confuse or irritate readers" (136), and theories that "posit the ideal of a stable, clear, and complete text" (137). These formulations, she contends, limit the potential meaning and practice of revision. That is, when we view revision as the management of meaning, we miss out on revision as a process of creating alternatives.

To understand revision as something more complex than a "stage" in a process model of composing, Welch draws on feminist psychoanalytic theory to develop a theory of revision that welcomes "dis-orientation" in the gaps between drafts. Such dis-orientation, she argues, enables writers to hear and contend with silences left unchecked in their previously "clear" versions. Welch's argument echoes those of other scholars in the field who invite us to reconsider the value of what she terms "real tight" essays, texts that foreground traditional notions of coherence and clarity at the expense of contradiction, disruption, and expanded points of view. Indeed, the arguments of those who advocate experimental writing prompt us to ask: What else might we, as writers and readers, learn if we risk writing in ways that foster dis-orientation rather than shut it down?

In a move toward answering this question, Welch concludes her book with a multigenre chapter titled, "Toward an Excess-ive Theory of Revision." Her purpose is to practice the revision theory she advocates in the rest of the book. As such she must necessarily break "real tight" form in order to dramatize for her readers the value of dis-orientation. She does so by defying "real tight" form on two levels: the textual and the theoretical. In both form and content, Welch transgresses boundaries by making connections across traditionally separated genres, authors, theories, and disciplines. For example, she juxtaposes academic essay with autobiography, self-authored fiction, student writing, students' reflections on their writing processes, and scenes from classroom and writing center conferences. She remembers her own experiences as a student in a fiction writing seminar as she reflects back on helping students write fiction. Throughout the chapter, Welch references the works of a wide variety of authors, including (but certainly not limited to) her students, rhetoric and composition scholars (e.g., Bartholomae, Flower, Bizzell, Spellmeyer), Lacan and Freud, psychoanalytic film theorist Joan Copjec, feminist theorists Jane Tompkins and Adrienne Rich, fiction writers Margaret Atwood, Maxine Hong Kingston, Tim O'Brien, and Paule Marshall, and poets T. Alan Broughton, Cornelius Early, and Adrienne Su.

By linking the theories and texts of these diverse writers, Welch creates a transgressive parlor room, a site in which she explores the boundaries of her students' texts, her own writing, as well as her interactions with other writers. Echoing the voices of contemporary feminist theorists, Welch explains that

> it's in the pursuit of what exceeds, what transgresses, what is restless and irritated, that we can locate the beginnings of identity, voice, and revision—revision as getting restless with a first draft's boundaries, revision as asking, 'Something missing, something else?' of our texts and our lives. (137)

For example, early in the chapter Welch introduces three revision narratives that "suggest why we need to address these issues of restlessness, confusion, and excess along the borders of convention and genre" (139). In each story, Welch describes how writers grapple with the tensions that result when the messiness of lived experience impinges on evolving draft. A first-year writing student named "Brandie," for example, struggles with a peer's suggestion to revise the corny tone of her personal narrative by including some darker emotions. Brandie responds by nodding and then saying, "'But I don't want to put any of that in the story. It would take away from the positive idea I'm trying to get across. I don't want people to think I'm a mess'" (140). In another story, a writing teacher talks about her stacks of unrevised and unsubmitted journal articles, texts she does not want to change because she does not "'want to take the life out of them'" (141). Afraid she might do to her students' essays what journal reviewers have done to her own, this teacher admits that she does not really know how to teach revision to students; she worries that directions to "clean up" their papers will kill the "life" that exists in earlier versions (140–41). For Welch, both these stories reveal the beginning of what she terms a "revisionary consciousness" (141), the awareness that "full, excessive lives" push against "the strict limits of texts that must be ironed out, made unwrinkled and smooth" (141). Welch argues that despite the discomfort produced by this pushing against, we as teachers, writers, and human beings act irresponsibly when we deny its existence. To deny this discomfort is to ignore the presence of dissenting voices, to refuse to hear and contend with difference. When we resolve the narrative neatly, we might feel satisfied, but we have failed to practice revision as a growing art.

Welch's revision narratives help construct the theoretical base—the content—that mirrors her form. In a classic feminist double-move, she creates through her essay's form the very conditions of discomfort she theorizes. Thus, as Welch explores the revisionary potential of writers pushing against the limits of their texts, she as writer pushes against the limits of her relationship with her reader. Her "restless" nonlinear essay form no doubt tests the limits of her academic reader's patience. Instead of offering traditional transitions,

Welch often punctuates sections with white space and a series of three asterisks. In her opening section, for example, Welch begins traditionally by reviewing existing theories of revision in the field, challenging them, and then questioning how teachers might teach a revised theory of revision. As such, she conforms to a standard form of the academic essay: Open with a review of the literature, follow with a discussion of the "problem," and conclude with an offer of something new and improved. Welch, however, breaks form and disrupts her readers' genre expectations by using white space and then opening her second part of this section as follows:

> My short story "The Cheating Kind" (1994) started with a memory from my teenage years: riding the backroads in an old, beat-up Cadillac that my best friend's father and his girlfriend loaned us along with a six-pack of Black Label beer because, even though we were only fifteen, without licenses, our presence wasn't wanted in the house. (137)

The text in this part, which continues with Welch's reflection on her process of writing it, is italicized, and therefore further visually distanced from the text that precedes it. Welch then includes a portion of the story itself, its ending, where the I-narrator and her best friend Marla are involved in a minor car accident:

> It was only slender stalks of corn, ripe and ready for the picking, that we hit. They gave way easily, and Marla, of course, didn't die. It would be an easier story to tell if she had—the stuff of high drama like Gatsby face down and bleeding in a pool, the romance of a steak knife shivering between two ribs. I couldn't simply walk away then, pretend it never happened, brush off my acquaintance with Marla like a fine layer of dirt. . . . (138)

The story continues and ends, Welch explains, when the middle-class narrator "leaves Marla with the wreck, Marla to take the blame, back to the quiet, polite, 'nothing-ever-happens-here' part of town" (138).

Welch's break in form is dramatic because she self-consciously juxtaposes two distinctly different genres, academic essay and fiction, within the boundaries of a single text—the scholarly chapter. But her text is something more than an example of experimental writing; it also demonstrates key principles of a relational rhetoric designed to promote better listening across a field of difference. The breaks between genres confuse the academic reader, who is then forced to slow down and listen to the silences, silences that ask her to examine the relationship between the genre conventions of this discipline and the academic identity they create. The academic we meet in the opening of the chapter (in a book published by Boynton/Cook as part of its series titled, CrossCurrents: New Perspectives in Rhetoric and Composition) is the rhetoric and composition scholar with whom most of us are familiar. Welch's references to other scholars and her rhetorical moves—review, problematize, suggest—are also familiar to her audience. But who is it that emerges after the space break? A *fiction* writer? This is a Nancy Welch I do not know, someone I did not get a chance to meet at the last 4Cs.

It is in this way that Welch's shift in genre signals a shift in academic identity. Performing this shift within the limits of a single text enables Welch to transgress disciplinary boundaries, blurring RhetComp and creative writing while simultaneously demonstrating to her readers that she, too, is a blurred subject. By positioning traditional academic essay alongside a self-authored work of fiction, Welch delays the linear progression of her argument; she switches genres on us, shattering our expectations of "what's next" and prompting us to listen better, to lean in and ask, "what is she doing, and why?" Clearly Welch wants us to know she writes fiction, that she's more than a scholar. Is her inclusion of the self-authored piece mere ego, or is she trying to do something more complex? These questions ran through my mind as I struggled with her space breaks and genre-switching. My understanding of Welch's rhetorical purpose began when I read and paused over an italicized passage that follows a psychoanalytic analysis of the ways composition scholars traditionally theorize revision. Welch opens this passage with a reference to Jane Tompkins's "Fighting Words: Unlearning to Write Critical Essays," and she explains how Tompkins challenges the way academics build their authority: by "gunning each other's readings down" (147). Welch then links Tompkins's analysis to the "narrative" of her own first academic publication:

> [S]et up this authority, set up that, then tear them down, get on with what you want to say. I was shaken when, one year later, I met one of those authorities face to face. It occurred to me then, and should have occurred to me before, that she was more than a few words on the page I chose to quote: a living breathing person leading a complex life, asking complex questions—who she is and what her work is far exceeding the boundaries I'd drawn. In this chapter, too, I'm doing it again, choosing quotations from writers whose work exceeds the space I'm giving them and the narrow focus of revision I've selected. This is a problem—one to which I keep returning, not skipping over with a gesture of a "However" or a "Yet it's easy to see . . .," creating a text that's problematically concise, simply clear. (147)

In this key passage, Welch's metadiscursive commentary enables her both to establish her scholarly authority as she critiques the very conventions of her authority-making. Rather than legitimize reductive and agnostic debate, Welch searches for other ways of building academic authority that do not involve simplifying the arguments and lives of others.

Viewed through the lens of this purpose, Welch's attention to multiple genres and the revisions they inspire takes on greater significance. By "migrating" into other programs within English departments and researching revision through the genres produced there, Welch finds new ways of building academic authority, one that welcomes the voices of colleagues working within and beyond the boundaries of RhetComp. For example, in one italicized passage, Welch writes about thinking over Tompkins's essay and its challenges as she reads poems by T. Alan Broughton that meditate on letters written by Vincent Van Gogh to his brother Theo, one by Cornelius Early written from a photograph of Dexter Gordon, another by Adrienne Su that takes its occasion from a sentence in *Alice's Adventures in Wonderland:* "Everything is queer today." Funny that poets are often charged with sequestering themselves in silent garrets or with suffering the most from the anxiety of influence. These three poets model for me ways of beginning to write, of working with the words of others, and of finding a voice—ways that don't involve setting up and knocking down. They suggest how we might revise our usual forms of academic production by remaining at, rather than trying to get past, that border between one's text and others. (150)

In each of her examples, Welch presents a poet who turns to another discipline—fine arts, photography, literature—to find an "occasion" out of which to write. This occasion, Welch explains, takes place on the border between academic programs, identities, and genres. She argues that by migrating to the border and staying put rather than rushing across, we can better contend with the complexities of a usefully transgressive English studies identity. More specifically, Welch holds that we, like the poets she cites, can put into practice a revised academic ethos, one where intertextuality is experienced as connection rather than dismissal. This move to connect with sources rather than put them down is characteristic of a rhetoric committed to establishing and maintaining relationship across differences.[2] To alter conventions, then—indeed, to change what it means to "cite your sources"—is more than a simple change in the way we research; as Welch explains, our reasons for citing as we do are tied to our notions of what it means to be a RhetComp scholar, and both should be open to revision. By way of illustration, Welch includes her own fiction along with substantial references to works by other creative writers, thereby challenging a RhetComp perspective that positions creative writing as romantic expressivism, a kind of "compositioning" with which RhetComp need not be concerned. Furthermore, by including creative writing in a book primarily concerned with the teaching of writing, Welch challenges her colleagues in creative writing to rethink the arbitrary boundaries they erect to distinguish between their writing and their *teaching* of writing. Indeed, through her own example, Welch makes clear that rereading one's scholarly and creative writing within a pedagogical context is an enormously useful way to problematize assumptions many professional writers hold about the differences between their writing and the writing their students produce.

Richard E. Miller's "The Nervous System" contains a series of "scenes" punctuated with white spaces and, within each space break, a single asterisk. Like the white space marking the indentation of a new paragraph, these breaks signify transition, movement, the emergence of new thought, the progression of argument. And yet Miller does not simply indent. He breaks form by refusing to offer the reader linear transitions that make obvious the progression of his argument. By mixing genres and his own subjectivities as a writer, Miller, like Welch, disrupts the belief that academic articles should be unified wholes. Instead, the gaps his weaving creates ask us to slow down so that we might hear him better.

In the essay, Miller argues for a revised notion of academic work, one that eschews an academic/personal binary and instead critically engages a "both/and" perspective. Through a series of compelling examples—from his own life, his teaching experiences, conference presentations, the media—Miller demonstrates how an academic/personal binary is problematic for two reasons. First, the common lament: Such a division separates that which is inextricably entwined. An academic context *is* a personal context for those who choose to teach and learn in the academy. Second, however, is his more interesting and subtle point: We have theorized how the personal has made its way into the academy, but we have yet to examine carefully how the academy has made its way into the private. Thus, Miller's essay is not a simple argument in favor of including personal narratives in scholarly work. Indeed, he has his own reservations about published stories that fail to give him "an idea to work with" (267). Instead, his essay is an attempt to read the body through the lens of public narratives—the body of the writer who feels something as he writes a poem about his troubled father, the writer who cries when he rereads his own work, the body of the reader who, sitting in a graduate student lounge, confronting a stack of unread issues of *College English,* reads the poem and cries, too.

Such a study of bodily reactions to "writing that matters" has scholarly significance on two levels. First, by examining what moves us, what makes us nervous, the kind of language that makes us sweat, we can more fully ponder questions such as, "Who is an academic? What does an academic value, find tasteful, distasteful, and why?" Furthermore,

> by studying the writer's response to composing at the moment of production, we can explore the relationship between modes of writing legitimated by the academy and the circulation of cultural capital in our society. Pursuing such an investigation, I believe, serves both a lexical and a pedagogical function: it allows us to widen the definition of what it means to write self-reflexively and it provides a way to index those places in the text where a true revision not only of the writer's argument but also of the writer's circumstance can occur. (273)

By listening to how our bodies respond in academic contexts, particularly during those times when they fall silent, Miller argues that we can understand how dominant disciplinary narratives lead us to speak about our personal experiences in ways that legitimize both the narratives and the identity they create.

As an example of how the academy's public narratives shape private experience, Miller describes a moment in a graduate teaching seminar when two gay teachers explained their reasons for deciding whether to come out in class. Their stories prompted other stories by other teachers, who, as Miller explains, "took the opportunity to deploy the structure of the coming out narrative to tell their own stories" (279), all of which somehow connected each teacher to the gay community. However, later in the seminar, the talk halted when another teacher "came out" as a Christian and described her own fears in the classroom. Miller reports that "no one knew what to say, so we took a break and came back to reflect on what had happened in the discussion and its aftereffects" (280). According to Miller, the first set of stories made way for more stories because they currently carry institutional capital. Members of the seminar were able to listen well because they knew their turn would come and they could speak back in ways that enabled them to be seen in the "right" light. While this desire to be seen, to tell the right kinds of stories so that we might be recognized, published, and promoted, is a practical necessity, Miller worries that such privileging limits the stories that can be told. By theorizing our responses to the second moment, those times when we do not speak because we do not know how our doing so will enable us to be seen well, Miller argues that we can more fully understand the assumptions and conventions on which an acceptable academic identity is built.

In addition to yielding useful knowledge about how we see ourselves as academics, exploring those moments when public narrative plays itself out in and on the body can help us find ways to listen to those people who do not follow the disciplinary script. To do so, Miller argues that we need to develop a multivocal fluency:

> an ability to hear things previously shut out or ignored, to attend to matters that might otherwise be overlooked or dismissed as irrelevant, to accept, in effect, the fact that learning to speak in such a way that one gets heard is a life-long project that involves, perhaps paradoxically, first learning how to listen better to others. (285)

Such fluency would help us listen to the struggles and fears of the Christian teacher in Miller's seminar. Our job in these contexts, explains Miller, "is not to listen for the speaker's mastery of a subject, but instead to acknowledge her presence, to attend to the minutiae of her life" (277).

Miller's essay demonstrates one way multigenre texts promote the practice of revisionary rhetoric. His multigenre form, with its frequent breaks and use of white space, serves the development of his argument because it refuses to reinforce the binary thinking he condemns. Miller dismantles the familiar personal/academic binary by refusing to play by its rules; instead he constructs an ongoing metadiscursive commentary that disrupts readers' attempts to pigeonhole his argument. "Is he for or against the personal in the academic?" I asked myself during my initial reading. In search of an answer, I paid special attention to how Miller begins his essay:

> For his second attempt, my father selected a set of kitchen knives and, when he got to the garage, a hammer from his toolbox. Shortly after my mother found him, the emergency crew rushed him to the hospital and the neighbors and the parish priest arrived to offer what services they could. Then, amidst the frenzied activity in the Intensive Care unit, my father struggled to explain the presence of the hammer. At a loss for words, he could only say that he had felt at the time that it "might have been of some use." (265)

Following this narrative and his theorizing of it, Miller adds this metadiscursive comment:

> On the one hand, then, we have the scene in the garage with the knives and the hammer, the rescue workers on their way, the ultimately, inaccessible, illegible event. On the other, the speaker at the podium, the performance of a masterful reading, the laughing crowd, the erasure of lived experience, the claim to possess truly useful knowledge. (266)

Here Miller acknowledges that, up to this point, his argument has been framed in familiar binary terms: There is the material body, the personal essayist, and then there is the conference presentation about the body, the academic. Because he begins with the narrative of his father's attempted suicide, and because his essay is titled "The

Nervous System," I thought I knew where Miller's loyalties lie: He
favors the personal over the disembodied academic and will side
with that camp as he continues to develop his argument.

In the very next section, however, Miller provides a series of
metadiscursive comments that challenge this simple reading:

> To stage the debate this way . . . is both to establish a fa-
> miliar set of oppositions and to guarantee an equally famil-
> iar outcome. That is, if I'm going to follow the generic con-
> ventions which I have been working with and which have
> been working with me up to this point, I must now argue
> for a return to the "personal" or "non-academic" writing
> as a way to reclaim a form of expression that really mat-
> ters—writing that reaches beyond the walls of conferences,
> that eschews jargon to make a bigger tent, that dismantles
> the sense that the writer is the master of her past or of all
> that she surveys. (266–67)

Because Miller opens with a moving scene about his father's attempted
suicide, I *expected* him to come out in favor of personal narratives in
academic contexts; I continued to read his essay as if he were opposed
to disembodied academic arguments. However, when Miller breaks
form and reflects on his decision to do so, he demonstrates how
genre—in this case, the genre of the personal narrative—creates
readerly expectations about how writers position themselves in relation to disciplinary arguments. By stepping back and telling me that
he knows I'm doing this, Miller illustrates how my reductive reading
has forced him into a corner that he refuses to occupy. His metadiscursive commentary thus demands that I examine how genre expectations shape the way I hear a writer's argument. Furthermore, his
commentary denies validity to the binary precisely because it disrupts it, thereby forcing me to recognize how I have been conform-
ing to its terms. As such, his commentary demonstrates his self-reflexivity as writer as it prompts my self-reflexivity as reader.

Miller again deploys this strategy later in his essay, when he
argues that "taste" and "distaste" are cultural constructions and that

academic readers who are repulsed by revelations of the personal must examine how they have been constructed *as academics* to read in such a fashion. Rather than simply write off such responses as "natural" and "appropriate" in a given context, Miller invites us instead to view visceral reactions as material for critical analysis. By attending to the emotions of writers and readers, Miller argues that we can "excavat[e] bodily responses for material evidence of the ways culture is present in the writer's very act of experiencing the composing process and in the reader's responses to the writer's text" (272–73). In a self-reflexive move, Miller then turns around and applies such a reading to the opening of his own essay:

> Obviously, one could commence such work by turning to the opening of this essay. For the moment, though, I am less interested in investigating the reader's visceral response to one kind of primal scene ("Oh no, he's not really going to talk about suicide and writing is he?" "I can sense a reference to Hemingway or Plath coming any minute now," and so on) than I am in pursuing the possibility that the writer's response, during the process of composing, might be a site at which to explore the relationship between modes of writing legitimized by the academy and the circulation of cultural capital in our society. (273)

By looking back on his own essay, Miller creates metadiscursive commentary that reveals his own self-reflexivity and demands the same from his readers. If, for example, you are one of the readers who was put off by his opening, Miller's ironic commentary forces you to contend with his argument more personally. In a way, he has singled you out and forced you to examine how you have been constructed so that you respond as you do. Similarly, his commentary forces me—someone who was attracted to his essay initially because of the moving personal revelation in the first paragraph—to examine how I have been shaped to embrace rebellious personal disclosure in academic contexts.

As a final example of Miller's metadiscursivity and the ways it encourages writerly and readerly self-reflexivity, I turn to his inclusion of a self-authored poem titled "Around the House." As in Welch's essay, Miller's self-authored creative writing problematizes a RhetComp/Creative Writing distinction as it demonstrates the revisionary potential of situating creative writing in pedagogical and theoretical contexts. The poem's speaker is a man remembering a series of scenes from his early youth. There are images of tulips "banging against each other" in an amphitheater constructed by his father for just that purpose; images of young children laughing and falling in backyard weeds are juxtaposed with images of a solitary boy, alone in his attic, using up four hundred matches "trying to start a fire that wouldn't start" (273–75). Miller offers us the poem and his reflections on its composition as an example of how academic narratives invade private memories. Rather than view the poem as some reflection of an authentic, private self, Miller sees it instead as an assemblage culled from memory, a memory the vagueness of which demands an organizing structure. For Miller, this structure is a public narrative, "a familiar tale of loss, loneliness, abandonment" (276). Thus, as the lone poet composes his past, the public narrative invades, giving shape and coherence to a barrage of images. The literary reader, who also plays a role in the public narrative—what twenty-first century reader does not?—reads the poem and, as Miller argues, calls in a host of psychoanalytic tropes to critique the poem's meaning from a safe, theoretical distance. Thus, Miller explains, the poem remains in the realm of the private: We move from the poet's private room to the speaker's private psychology. What this kind of reading fails to provide us with is any sense of how the writer/reader experiences the intrusion of the public narrative on the private psyche.

To move us in the direction of theorizing this intersection, Miller helps us hear the body by reflecting on his own process of composing the poem. He tells us that he was "overwhelmed with grief" (273) while writing, that tears streamed down his face as he crafted the lines "I can see you. I can hear you" (276). What are we, as readers trained in the art of close reading, to make of these bodily disruptions and Miller's revelation of them? It is, in fact, his revelation of personal grief that he supposes will bring discomfort to more than a few of his own readers. The public narrative of loss and abandonment invades and organizes the poet Miller's memory, prompting grief and tears. In turn, Miller the academic essayist offers us his grief and tears not *as* poem, not *as* private, authentic experience but instead as symptoms of a shared cultural story. Miller recreates for his readers a version of his own discomfort while composing. When theorized in these terms, our reading of his poem and his reading of the poem's effects render it impossible for us to step outside the story without having been touched. While we may not feel overwhelmed with grief as we read, we are certainly made to feel *something,* whether it be revulsion at his lack of appropriate scholarly taste or a pang in the gut. Furthermore, Miller's demands for self-reflexivity force us to acknowledge those feelings, to attend to them, and to consider how they are the result of a disquieting clash between private memory and legitimized public narrative.

By denying truth to a familiar set of oppositions, Miller's metadiscursive commentary creates a space for a third way, a way out of the personal/academic binary, a new way to think about the two terms without immediately placing them in opposition to one another. His commentary does so by spurring self-reflexivity in both himself as writer and in the reader. He questions his own moves as rhetor as he demands that readers examine their own attempts to fit his argument into a safe and comfortable set of disciplinary conventions. Indeed, Min-Zhan Lu's response to Miller's essay evinces this claim. In her critique of Miller's essay, she uses her initial response to it as a springboard to demonstrate the revisionary power of what she terms "critical affirmation," a literate process committed to social justice, one that has "the following goals":

> (1) To end oppression rather than to empower a particular form of self, group, or culture; (2) To grapple with one's privilege as well as one's experience of exclusion; (3) To approach more respectfully and responsibly those histories

and experiences which appear different from what one calls
one's own; and (4) To affirm a yearning for individual agency
shared by individuals across social divisions without losing
sight of the different material circumstances which shape this
yearning and against which each of us must struggle when
enacting such yearning. ("Redefining," 173)

In an effort to practice this form of literacy, Lu rereads several texts
through its lens, one of which is Miller's essay. His essay bothers her
for two reasons. First, in his citation of a quotation by Cornel West,
Miller deletes a modifier in which West references the abilities of
"black foremothers and forefathers" to survive self-annihilation. For
Lu, this citation practice is problematic because "it risks losing sight
of what 'the history of black America' has to offer us on how to combat self-annihilation in a culture where deep economic, cultural, and
political problems have been allowed to fester for decades" (182; ref-
erencing West). Second, Lu critiques Miller's "tendency to explicitly
describe only those who are 'black' as having racial identities, without similarly marking or considering his own racial identity" (182).

Rather than engage in the discipline's "conventions of attack/
counter-strike" (182), however, Lu chooses instead to revise her
initial response to Miller's essay by critically affirming the ways in
which she, too, has deployed the same rhetorical moves that disturb her. In the remainder of her essay, she does just that, turning
"the critical gaze on [her] own action" (184) to problematize her
"tendency to conflate the history of all racially oppressed groups"
(185). Lu's essay is a dramatic example of one reader's efforts to own
responsibly her reactions to a text that disturbs her. My purpose in
discussing it here, however, is to suggest the degree to which Miller's
multigenre form encourages such a response. In fact, Lu herself
identifies three types of response she could have written but decided
against. The first would have been to situate Miller's troubling rhetorical gestures within a context that holds his political intents sus-
pect. He is, after all, a white, heterosexual male with considerable
standing in the field. Another would have been to "treat the moves
as evidence of the writer's intellectual limitations" (182). A third

would have been to keep her responses private out of fear that her criticisms would have been heard as attempts to undermine "the very sort of coalition-building [she is] interested in promoting" (183). Instead of responding in these predictable ways, however, Lu chooses to do something else; her decision to do so results in a sophisticated theory of listening to difference.

It is in this sense, then, that metadiscursivity and self-reflexivity fuel revision: By looking back on ourselves and our arguments, by being put in a position of having to ask, "what am I doing and why?" we ask questions previously left unasked, and we hear answers that change our texts and our world.

> As readers, we need to be equally vigilant towards the ways in which the either/or mentality sets us in motion, urging us to operate as butterfly collectors fixated on reducing and displaying the position of the writer at the cost of ignoring the writer's often complex and alternative textual moves as well as the writer's complex, dynamic relations to the world.
> —Min-Zhan Lu, "Reading the Personal"

Both Welch and Miller use multigenre forms to facilitate their theorizing of productive discomfort. Their revisionary rhetorical strategies, which put us in the position of experiencing discomfort, demand that we look at our own tendencies to pigeonhole others, to "clean up" messes by resorting to convenient but reductive binaries. For both, writing in multiple genres disrupts this readerly tendency; doing so also makes heard the ways in which disciplinary values are reflected in generic conventions. By migrating to new genres, these writers prevent us from pigeonholing them as they invite us to see ourselves and our discipline anew. Both help us envision ways we might find value in that which does not "fit in," whether it be the opinions of Christian colleagues or students' dark emotions or RhetComp scholars who dream of writing poetry.[3] When read together, Miller and Welch expose the binary logic informing our academic identity: If we listen to be seen, and if being seen is founded on arguing against, then we have no choice but to listen reductively. Because rhetoric and composition studies in some sense has always been a discipline that does not quite "fit in," and indeed because many of us see ourselves as misfits, it makes sense that it is we who might forge new ways of listening, new strategies for fostering cross-boundary discourse. Although there is pain in not belonging, we need to recognize we have had a hand in shaping our outsider status. It is here, on the borders of belonging, that revisionary work gets done.

3 / Putting the Wrong Words Together
Disrupting Narratives in English Studies

When I was in the second grade, I caused, among other things, a food fight in the school cafeteria. I attended a well-funded public school in suburban Ohio, which, at that time (the early 1970s), was interested in expanding the perspectives of its largely white, middle-class student body. Grade levels, and units within them, for example, were named after American Indian tribes. In the second grade, I was a Cherokee. Admittedly, my understanding of Cherokee culture was not expanded much beyond where they used to live, how they used to dress, and what they used to eat. And there was certainly no inquiry into the discourse of "used-to"-ness. But I did have the good luck of attending speech therapy three times a week, where my therapist—an American Indian and self-professed hippie artist—would talk with me about culture and politics, oppression and social activism, and sometimes correct my pronunciation along the way. It was during this time that I noticed our school cafeteria was segregated, with boys on one side and girls on the other. Because no one had ever told me I could not sit with the boys, I decided one day to do just that.

What I remember next—and here memory gets fuzzy and no doubt embellished—what I remember next is a disruption unlike any I had ever seen in school. Boys started screaming; some of them fell out of their seats. At one point somebody started throwing food.[1] Shortly thereafter the principal, Mr. Schenking, joined me at the boys' table and asked me if I would please go back to the other side. Because the consequences of my decision had been so unexpected and therefore so scary, I agreed. Like Mr. Schenking, I wanted order restored, and quickly. I never sat on the boys' side again.

In *Permanence and Change*, Kenneth Burke defines metaphor as a process of "putting the wrong words together" (91), a move which reconceives metaphor as dramatistic motive rather than static trope. It is through such a process, Burke continues, that people are able to attain pliancy in their thinking, a flexibility needed to make room for expanded points of view. In my own work, the insights afforded by Burkean metaphor have come to represent what I mean by *revision*, the jarring consequence of putting those wrongs words together what I mean by *disruption*. I argue that disruption must precede revision if what we seek is change on the level of attitude.

But disruption isn't enough; it is only a first step. As my narrative above demonstrates, my decision to put two wrong words together—boys and girls—certainly created disruption, but it did not result in changed attitudes and revised perspectives. If anything, the disruption legitimized the status quo by reaffirming the commonplace that, yes, indeed, boys and girls of a certain age should be kept apart.

To be sure, I am not saying they shouldn't. God knows I have never taught hordes of eight-year-olds. What I'm lamenting, however, is the unexplored revisionary moment made possible by that lunchroom disruption. Why did the girls and boys so "naturally" sit on different sides? What did the boys' reaction to my joining them signify? How was this related to my choice to sit next to one of only two African American males in my class? What can be made of my quick decision to restore and maintain order?[2] The aftermath of disruption holds the possibility of a revisionary consciousness. Its emergence depends on our willingness to ask critically intervening questions of each other and ourselves.

In this chapter, I describe a multigenre reflective narrative assignment designed to help students listen more fully to the unexplored revisionary moments in their own rough drafts. Initially, my primary goal was to analyze the ways in which student writers use genre migrations to construct different and sometimes contradictory subject positions as English majors. However, during the process of writing about my students' texts and revision processes, I experienced a revisionary discomfort of my own I had not anticipated. More specifically, as I reread students' multigenre texts, which necessarily included genres that extended beyond the borders of my self-perceived area of expertise, I was challenged to rethink *my* subject position(s) as English teacher. Listening to this discomfort afforded me the opportunity to ask critically intervening questions about the teacherly subject positions(s) I constructed in response to students' texts. Consequently, this chapter also includes a discussion of the ways in which multigenre writing can create disciplinary tensions for teachers whose students begin writing in "non-RhetComp" genres.

Authorizing Student Disruption

I developed a multigenre reflective essay assignment (see Appendix A) to authorize student disruption in an effort to promote students' practice of revisionary rhetoric.[3] In general, such an assignment illustrates one way teachers can position *reflection* as something other than personal revelation or guilt-ridden self-critique.[4] Explaining the limitations of theorizing reflection in these terms, Min-Zhan Lu argues:

> [I]n teaching and research, "personal experience" is often treated as a self-evident thing existing prior to and outside of discursive practices. Personal narratives are thus viewed as a direct reflection of the writing self and her culture. "Experience" is seldom explored as a process we can only have access to discursively, through the mediation of a complex network of power, desire, and interests. Nor is it usually treated as a possible site for critical intervention on the formation of one's self and the material conditions of one's life. Thus, recitation and revelation rather than revision remain the dominant modes of writing the personal. ("Redefining," 174)

However, when reflection is understood as a mode of personal writing that practices rhetorical listening, it emerges instead as a process through which a listener speaks back, thereby giving voice to—and becoming publicly responsible for—the ways in which she has heard others. Concerned equally with constructions of self, reflection also emerges "as a trope for interpretive invention that applies not just to the discourses of others but also to the discourses of one's self" (Ratcliffe, 219). In other words, it is through reflection that a listener-turned-speaker becomes both able and obligated to interrogate discursive constructions of self and other.

The multigenre assignment is ideally suited to the practice of rhetorical listening because it authorizes students to reflect on texts—and the subjectivities of the authors who produced them—that are often excluded in academic contexts. By making such inclusions possible, the assignment especially speaks to those students who can often find no other acceptable setting to reflect on those subject positions that conflict with the authorial position of the professor and the institution s/he represents. Describing the ideological conflicts working-class college students frequently experience, bell hooks, for example, observes that many students drop out because they are unable to resolve the contradictions that exist between the values and belief systems needed in order to "make it" with those that are embraced at home (*Teaching*, 182). According to hooks, these students become passive and feel victimized, thinking they have only two choices: accept the dominant ideology or reject it. To push them beyond this binary, hooks counsels them to "creatively invent ways to cross borders" (*Teaching*, 183). The multigenre reflective essay not only takes the burden of creative invention off the shoulders of these students, it also positions border crossing as a legitimate academic activity.

Furthermore, by requiring students to draft essays that juxtapose genres usually kept separate, both students and teachers can look for places in the narrative where students temporarily abandon one genre and migrate to something else. Such pivots suggest the desire to voice a subject position that exceeds the boundaries of genre, discipline, and institution.[5] Consequently, these pivots—these disruptions in reflective narrative coherence—promote a conceptual pliancy necessary for deep, attitudinal revision. Finally, because the multigenre reflective essay facilitates students' ability to listen "for the exiled excess" (Ratcliffe, 203) in their narratives, the assignment also disenables the "easy" responses of unexamined identification or defensive critique.

I assigned a version of a multigenre reflective essay assignment for the first time to my students enrolled in English 300—Senior Seminar—in Spring 2001. A required capstone course for English majors, Senior Seminar is a space where students reflect on their tenure as English majors by analyzing the (dis)connections they experienced across their English studies courses (rhetoric and composition, creative writing, linguistics, and literature). Students in every section prepare a portfolio that contains sample texts written in each of their English courses. Typically, students also write a reflective letter that introduces these contents and describes their development as English majors. In my class, I eliminated this second requirement and instead asked students to prepare, as their final project for their course, a multigenre reflective essay. I did so because I have read too many reflective portfolio letters that read as simplified stories of progress and success. These narratives often lack the complexities of contradiction, conflict, and difference—the disruptions that make deep revision possible. My hope was that the multigenre reflective essay would supply these disruptions and thus compel students to construct a narrative that went beyond a simplified account of "what happened" during their years as English majors. Instead, I wanted the assignment to foster students' ability to analyze critically their participation in the field of English studies. I hoped that by listening rhetorically to the ways in which they had been and were currently being "disciplined," my students would be able to critically affirm their investment in discursive constructions of disciplinary identity. In addition, I hoped my students' reflections would challenge *my* identity as a member of the discipline, a process I anticipated would require me to listen rhetorically and revise accordingly.

In the following two analyses of student writing, I attempt to do just that. I chose these students' texts because each of them demonstrates the insights that accrue when wrong words are put together. Respectively, these students put *English* together with *death* and *sin*.

English and Death
Heather[6] is a white, middle-class, 22-year-old college senior who became an English major only after experimenting with business,

journalism, history, and psychology. In her multigenre reflective essay, Heather uses her knowledge of psychology to analyze the way in which her personal life "subconsciously" emerges in her academic writing. This need for a personally expressive outlet she locates in the fact that she never gave herself the opportunity to write for herself about herself. As Heather explains:

> I never had a diary or journal, because I had two brothers, one older and one younger. There was nothing secret or sacred in my house, so I never had the chance to see how writing can be a way of expression, and not just a tool to receive desired grades.

She arrives at this conclusion after juxtaposing texts produced in her English classes—which combine her interest in psychology with her growing awareness of feminist theory—with a membership form to Gold's gym and increasingly larger-sized tags from her jeans. Reading across these texts, Heather observes the degree to which her concerns about weight and fitness found academic legitimacy in several different English courses. In a research paper written in first-year composition, for example, she chooses to write about eating disorders. A few years later, while enrolled in introductory creative writing, she produces a story about a girl struggling with anorexia nervosa. And in my class, which requires students to revise a text from a previous course, Heather chooses to retell the eating disorder story from the perspective of the girl's mother. Although Heather never announces that she herself has an eating disorder, she does write that "[t]his area of my life is persistent in trying to resolve itself through my writing."

In another instance, Heather finds greater closure while reflecting on her reasons for writing "Why Wait," a text she produced in her Advanced Composition class:

> [W]hen I wrote "Why Wait," I thought I was stating perfectly good reasons why I did not want to get married yet, and explained why the constant engagement of others was

not helping my pressure situation. However, I was simply
writing down my insecurities and my own excuses. I
wanted to get married, to start the process of growing up
and taking on new responsibilities, but I was not in a position to do that, because I was still in college. I did not
know how to take those first few steps into adulthood and
responsibility land while I was still stuck in the limbo land
of college.

Now, as a college senior about to graduate, Heather is able to reread this paper, challenge its logic, and conclude: "I was not ready
[then] to accept my feelings and that is how they ended up in an
academic paper."

Using the reflective process as a means to uncover and resolve
personal problems buried in academic texts is a focusing theme in
Heather's essay. Indeed, her very title. "I Found Myself in My Writing," evinces her commitment to the belief that personal revelation
is a necessary step in the construction of self. Furthermore, in ex-
ceeding the boundaries of traditional academic writing by unconsciously importing personal themes, Heather suggests that this is a
self that cannot construct itself publicly, at least not in academic contexts. Instead, it is a self that must be uncovered, revealed.

This thematic confidence/coherence continues until page 8,
when it is disrupted by the following:

I now come to my final year of school and I do not know
what to say. Last semester I had semantics, and in that class
we spent a lot of time trying to make sense of our language,
our place in [college], our lives, and basically we tried to
make sense of meaning. Yet, *sometimes looking back is not
the way to do that* (emphasis added).

This summer my dad was diagnosed with cancer. The
tumor was inside his spine, and therefore un-removable or
as the doctors called it, inoperable. Over spring break, we
took him to the hospital, because he was having trouble
breathing. There the doctors told us he had through the

weekend to live. He died in his bed, next to my mom on
March 11, 2001, at 6:10 in the morning. My life and studies and writings all changed. Everyone brings themselves
to their writing with all their experiences. And that is why
I am about to write what comes next.

For this project we are supposed to analyze what kind
of student the English department is producing, but I do
not know how to do that. Sure, we have all learned skills
to go into different texts and analyze them through a variety of aspects, but what we really have here is a group of
people that develop the English department and not vice
versa. The professors here do teach and tone our skills, but
they do not produce us.

This section interests me because in it I see Heather challenging her
own focusing theme as well as the assignment itself. First, there is
the line I have italicized: *Sometimes looking back is not the way to do
that.* In other words, sometimes reflecting on our experiences—no
matter how critically—does not help us make sense of our lives.
Indeed, when looking back means remembering the death of someone we love, reflection simply means more confusion, more sense-
less loss. This is precisely the insight rendered in Heather's admission that *she doesn't know what to say* in her final year of school, an
admission that signals discursive ownership of a revised reflective
self. This self who does not know appears in marked contrast to the
one whose reflections reveal itself *to* itself. Furthermore, Heather's
ability to construct a self who does not know is the paradoxical
consequence of her *intentional* revelation of the personal. The experience of her father's death is not filtered through research paper,
fiction, or logical narration; as a "personal problem" that will never
be "resolved," it stands alone, stark and unsentimental.

By publicly constructing a personal self that does not hide behind traditional academic genres, Heather disrupts her own reflective narrative. She can no longer sustain the unproblematized assertion that through reflection her life makes sense. It is this
disruption in both theme and sense of self that authorizes Heather

to "write what comes next"—namely, a rejection of the very assumption on which I built the course. Having constructed a public self that is able to say, "I don't know," Heather announces that she does not know how to complete the assignment as it was designed. This is not an admission of ignorance or incompetence. Instead, it is a challenge to my semester-long claims that my students, as English majors, were being disciplined—that is, produced—by the field and the institution. Countering that it is, in fact, the students—and not the professors—who produce the discipline, Heather counsels me to consider the ways in which *I* am produced by my students. In so doing, she not only reasserts a self who does know, she also revises her construction of me as teacher. I am no longer the authority I once was; instead, as someone capable of making faulty assumptions, I am like the students I profess to teach: people whose learning depends on challenges from others. This revision of me accompanies Heather's reinvention of herself—she is now someone who *poses* problems rather than uncovers or resolves them.

Had the semester not ended, I would have asked Heather to use this problem-posing self to interrogate the assumptions on which the first half of her essay rests. More specifically, I would have pushed her to situate both her obsession with weight and her contradictory attitudes toward marriage within the contexts of constructed social identities rather than revealed personal problems.

English and Sin

No other essay in my teaching career has generated more discomfort than Jeff's, "Seven Scholarly Sins."[7] Written in response to the assignment described earlier, Jeff uses the project as an opportunity to indict the institution, the discipline, and the majority of its teachers and students by ironically confessing the "sins" for which he is guilty: Impatience, Conservatism, Deceit, Doubt, Respect, Argumentation, and Ambition. On first reading, several of these "sins" surprised me, given that I assume the institution/discipline *wants* students to develop their argumentative skills and to do so ambitiously while remaining respectful of others. Furthermore, in my classes, I encourage students to let go of certainty and explore their doubts, framing inconclusivity as a conduit to expanded points of view. The "sin" of conservatism is less surprising, as I frequently encounter students whose religious and/or political ideologies run counter to those expressed in the assigned readings. The "sins" of impatience and deceit are less obviously ironic, as I think most people consider them to be character flaws, if not sins per se. Nevertheless, for Jeff, all seven attributes are "sinful" because they "go against the grain of higher learning."

Framing all these "sins," of course, is the eighth unspoken one—the "sin" of identifying as a religious person in a secular institution, as someone who sees people as being capable of committing things called sins, for which they must atone or be punished. In this way, then, Jeff's very title performs the disruption of Burkean metaphor: put together, "scholarly" and "sin" force us to ask: In academic contexts, in English classes, who are the sinners? Who is God? How does s/he punish? How does s/he judge? These questions suggest the rhetorical sophistication of Jeff's title, given that his purpose in much of his essay is to question institutional and professorial authority. For example, toward the end of his opening section, Jeff disrupts his first-person reflective narrative with dramatic dialogue to reconstruct the following argument he had with an unnamed departmental authority over a required course:

> "I have taken seven English classes before coming to this university. Clearly I can write."
> "But this is an introduction to English studies," I was told.
> "Great, such as?"
> "Well, rhetoric, son."
> "All right, but if you see on my transcripts I just had a rhetoric course that I did very well in."
> "Never-the-less, son, you have to take it."

While it is a common lament among students that a required course should not be required for *them*, what interests me is Jeff's migration to dialogue to dramatize a scene he could have chosen to retell through the reflective voice already established in the narrative. By using dialogue instead, Jeff is able to construct and give voice to one version of authority for which he has contempt—the voice of unreasonable, benevolent paternalism. Furthermore, Jeff's responses to this authority offer two versions of himself: the skillful rhetor, someone capable of making sound arguments (assuming the audience is a thinking one); and the derisive student ("Great, such as?"), someone whose past experiences with institutional bureaucracy make him suspicious of its supposed altruistic intentions.[8]

The remainder of Jeff's project demonstrates the creative strategies he uses to intersect these two subjectivities in ways that do not threaten his tenuous position as a student in classrooms where authorities have the power to fail him. For example, in his section on the "sin" of conservatism, Jeff explains how he secured a job as an editorial columnist with the college paper in an effort to voice his political opinions, arguments he was not willing to make in classes presided over by "left-wing" professors. Although his job with the paper took a lot of time and paid low wages, and although he already worked two other jobs to pay the bills, Jeff relished the extra work: "I was allowed to voice my opinion, and to get it out to the people who never were able to hear me during a discussion. I made it through my classes a little easier, because Friday was coming, and I could say everything I wanted to say in class in my column."[9] And, he adds, he was able to sleep at night. In his project Jeff includes as an example a column he wrote that condemns President Clinton for lying, abusing his power, and "lowering the moral tone" of the presidency.

This theme of contemptible authority appears in nearly every one of the texts Jeff chooses to juxtapose with his reflective narrative. In his section on respect, for example, he includes his evaluation of a math professor who assumed students' access to lab computers outside of class (which, with his three jobs, Jeff did not). The implication here is that Jeff is guilty of the sin of *expecting to be respected,* rather than being respectful, per se. In his section on the "sin" of lying, Jeff includes this narrative reflection:

I was born into an (upper) lower-middle type class family. My father worked hard on a steel worker's salary to send my brothers and sisters to good Catholic schools. It is said that all lower class types lie to make themselves appear upper-middle class. Big deal, right? I have never been ashamed of where I came from; in fact, I am proud of my father, and I am proud to call myself his son. No, I do not lie about things that others at this university lie about. I lie about my intelligence.

According to Jeff, because he does not spend a long time writing his papers, and because he does fairly well on them, he is an effective rhetor—he has persuaded his professors to believe that he is intelligent. (Curiously, it does not seem to occur to Jeff that it takes a great deal of intelligence to do just that.) To support this claim, Jeff attaches a response paper written in an upper-division literature course, where, for the sake of the grade, he fools the professor and renders an interpretation with which he does not agree and about which he does not care. This is what Jeff means, I believe, when he says he is guilty of lying. Interestingly, the response paper is a cultural critique of the working class as represented in Victorian literature. With this juxtaposition of texts—a narrative reflection on his own working-class background situated alongside a critique of literary representations of the working class—Jeff positions himself outside the community of liberal scholars he disdains. The ethical appeal established in the narrative suggests his ability to forge an interpretation of working-class representations about which he *does* care. However, because this interpretation would no doubt clash with the liberal agenda of his professor, Jeff decides to "lie." By ironically casting this lie as a scholarly "sin," Jeff calls into question assumptions made about members of the working class while simultaneously mocking professors who praise his shoddy work simply because it echoes these very assumptions.

While each of the juxtaposed texts addresses issues of authority and power, all of them are situated within a reflective narrative principally concerned with the complexities of belonging. In his opening remarks, Jeff positions himself as someone who does not belong. In fact, his first sentence reads: "As my time at a university where I do not belong comes to a close, the only thoughts which cross my mind are why? Why did I come to a university?" In an effort to answer this question, Jeff explains that he knew he wanted to write, and he thought perhaps a college education would help him do so. Because he idealized his post-college life as a hermit writing books in the woods, he joined the National Guard, thereby avoiding the burden of having to repay costly school loans. The physical and mental hardships of basic training fueled his desire to go college: "I thought college would be great. A group of people who actually wanted to be in school and learn and be motivated and be intelligent and be insightful." When he finally did experience higher education—first at a community college and then a university—Jeff was disappointed:

> I realized that I did not belong. These children were mainly attending extended high school to please their parents. I could not interact with them. I could not find something to say to include myself in their conversations. I realized that basic training had made me mature beyond my years.

This passage contains a tension Jeff sustains throughout his essay: On one hand, he feels he does not belong because he is unable to connect with other students. On the other hand, he does not *want* to belong if belonging means connecting with students he views as "children," "mindless and conformist totalitarians" who work outside of school not because they need money to eat, as Jeff does, but because they must "support their newfound alcohol addictions." They are "mindless schlubs" who "commute from sheltered suburban life or country life to a world within itself which they think they run because their parents have money and the school will do anything to keep that flow of money coming in." These students have "purchased a persona" and disrupted his studies with their "Friday night love fantasies told to their fraternity brothers." By constructing his peers in this manner, Jeff is able to pull off the reversal upon which his essay—and indeed, his identity—hinges: Belonging in a university community means truly wanting to learn. As the studious Other to his frat party peers, Jeff redefines the conditions of belonging. It is now he who belongs, and his peers who do not.

Jeff's contempt for his peers is disturbing, not just because he makes sweeping generalizations and so vehemently distances himself from those he could try harder to understand, but because he so eerily echoes sentiments expressed by my colleagues, conversations within which I also participate. As I write this, I remember the time Jeff and I were talking about his plans after graduation. He had asked me to write him a letter of recommendation for graduate school, and I was curious to know if he wanted to be a professor. He shook his head vigorously, looking around the now empty classroom. "I don't want to teach these people," he said. I remember I laughed, and then said, "Oh, come on. They're not *that* bad." In that moment, I could have challenged Jeff. I could have reminded him that many of the students in our class had made public the financial strains they were under, pressures that made learning difficult. I could have defended those students I have had the privilege to teach, motivated and committed learners who worked hard and contributed so much to my own education. Instead, I opted to align myself against them and with Jeff, our shared contempt for those nameless "schlubs" connecting us in a mutual struggle to belong somewhere *else*.

Listening to My Laughter

After my first few readings of Jeff's essay, I decided an analysis of it was ill-suited to this chapter. After all, it does not effectively demonstrate how students can listen for those subject positions too often marshaled to the excesses of academic (con)texts in order to interrogate discursive constructions of self and other. That is, while Jeff effectively challenges the ways others have constructed him, he examines neither his discursive constructions of himself nor the students and authorities he disdains. In short, he fails to practice rhetorical listening. However, given that I am advocating the revisionary potential of texts that produce readerly discomfort, I opted to include it.

My discomfort, of course, is tied to my position as Jeff's teacher. More specifically, I am embarrassed that I was unable to help Jeff reread his rough draft in a way that obligated him to take responsibility for his representations of himself, his teachers, and his peers. Certainly, the mindless bureaucrat and drunken frat boy are stereotypes I should have spotted sooner. However, rather than wallow in my embarrassment, I choose to listen rhetorically to my analysis of Jeff's essay, with the goal being to understand how and why I was unable to lead him to do the same.

I begin by situating my subject position as teacher alongside Jeff's as student. Jeff was given this assignment by me in a class I taught, and his essay was therefore read and assessed by me. Given what Jeff believes about teachers' power to fail and his need to "lie" and reroute arguments he cares about to his weekly newspaper column, I am moved to ask, Why was Jeff willing to write what he did? Perhaps because he was in his last semester, Jeff no longer worried about getting a bad reputation among professors within the department. However, because the course is required for graduation, Jeff still took a big risk in writing what he did, especially since the essay was worth 50 percent of his grade. Of course, he probably knew I would not fail him simply because we sometimes disagree. And, in fact, this is precisely the favorable view of myself that this reading reaffirms: I am an open-minded thinker, a teacher who is able and willing to create a space for arguments that challenge her own. While I admit to feeling comforted by this reading, I also realize feeling comfortable is not my goal. I am looking for something more, something else.

I try again.

According to Ratcliffe, we listen rhetorically when we "proceed from within a *responsibility* logic," a "performance" that "locate[s] identification in the discursive spaces of both *commonalities* and *differences*" (204, emphasis in original). In terms of our commonalities, neither Jeff nor I wants to be the university's pawn, uncritically adopting the personae we believe it is trying to sell us. For Jeff, this means resisting the identity of a boozing frat boy who sleeps through class dreaming of the next kegger. For me, it means resisting the identities of both benevolent bureaucrat and contemptible authority. Both of us position ourselves outside some university communities in order to include ourselves within two others: (1) a community of committed writers and (2) a community of scholars dedicated to the pursuit of knowledge.

Interestingly, it is by naming these commonalities that I am able to locate one of our glaring differences: presumably, as a university professor, I *already belong* to the communities I seek. Why, then, in the conversation with Jeff described earlier, did I let go unchallenged his statement that he does not want to "teach these people"? One answer, of course, is that my subject position as teacher requires the presence of subject positions called students. If teachers are scholars dedicated to the pursuit of knowledge, then students must be . . . drunken frat boys who sleep through class dreaming of the next kegger? I hope not. Such logic is founded on the kind of binary construction revisionary rhetoric seeks to disrupt.

Another, more useful answer results when I consider Bakhtin's concept of the superaddressee, which Frank Farmer explains as follows: "[W]ithin every utterance there is a presumed *third* listener, one beyond the addressee, or second listener, to whom the utterance is immediately addressed" (21, emphasis in the original). According to Farmer, Bakhtin refers to the superaddressee as the loophole addressee because

> the speaker (or author) can ill afford to "turn over his whole self and his speech work to the complete and final will of the addressees who are on hand or nearby" (*SG* 126–27). The risk here for the speaker (or author) is not only that what he or she says will be misunderstood, but rather that what is said will be misunderstood *utterly* and *forever.* The super-addressee thus offers a loophole for a perfect understanding *elsewhere* and a hedge against the dangers of a consummated misunderstanding *here.* (22, emphasis in original)

As speakers/writers, imagining the existence of a superaddressee gives us hope that we will, at some point, be heard and understood. Farmer continues that students who refer to their teachers in the third person are invoking both an immediate listener and a super-addressee, a double audience of teacher (the "one spoken *of*") and reader (the "one spoken *to*") (44, emphasis in original). Farmer locates this argument within an analysis of a paper written by his student Devlyn, who, like Jeff, writes an essay that indicts professorial authority:

> In Bakhtin's terms, the person referred to as 'Dr. Farmer' is the hero of Devlyn's discourse, its central theme to which Devlyn is oriented in an obviously evaluative way. But the other Dr. Farmer, the one actually reading Devlyn's essay, it would seem, is enlisted as an ally who will stand alongside Devlyn in his many grievances against the named 'Dr. Farmer' who appears in his essay. Again, using Bakhtinian terms, we might be tempted to say that Dr. Farmer, the reader, constitutes a *superaddressee* audience for Devlyn, an ideal but necessary third party, who will be responsive to his complaints, his request for the sort of fair hearing that Dr. Farmer, the teacher, could not or would not provide. (44)

Because Devlyn's paper reminded me so much of Jeff's, I decided to return to Jeff's, rereading it, looking for any places where he might have referred to me in the third person. My purpose was to see if and where Jeff invoked me as both enemy and ally, a passage wherein Jeff located his identification with me in terms of our commonalities and our differences.

I found a third person reference to me twice—one in his section on "Doubt," the other in the following section on "Respect." In "Doubt," Jeff includes a copy of an essay he wrote a few years earlier in his Advanced Composition class, where he questions the selection process used by the editor of a *Best American Essays* volume. Jeff doubts some of these selections, wondering if in fact they qualified as "the best." To make matters more interesting, Jeff took this class with me, the person who selected the text he critiques. In an essay written for that class, Jeff refers to me in third person as follows:

> I don't know if we actually understand that of which we gather three times a week for. We . . . one, two, three, eighteen of us—we meet, rather promptly, scheduled, as instructed. We stare into our outlets, our computers that is, until our mediator enters, and sees us properly to a beginning. She, young—unruly. Her position, one of envy among the newly found English majors with whom she involves.

Later in the essay, Jeff extends his questioning of what makes an essay "good" to a how an essay can be graded: "If the essay is so free—how the grade? How the direction?" In my end comment on his draft, I wrote the following:

> Jeff, I enjoyed reading this critique of the selection and evaluation process, both in *Best American Essays* and in my class. You ask good questions, and I find myself wanting to hear some of *your* answers to them. If something is blurred and out of reach, does that mean we can't grasp for it, and in our grasping, define, evaluate, critique, just as you do here? I think it's okay—even necessary—to evaluate, but I also believe . . . .

My end comment continues to the works cited page, which Jeff chooses not to photocopy and include in his project. Consequently, I am not sure how I ended that sentence, but I probably said something about the criteria for evaluation being open to dialogue and revision. In the margin next to where he describes me as young and unruly, I have written, "ha!"

Using Farmer's analysis as a model, I can read Jeff's third-person reference to me as an attempt to show Julie-the-reader how Julie-the-teacher was viewed by at least one of her students: She was envied for the power she held; her youth and unruliness were unusual enough to deserve mention; she was a "mediator," not a "professor" or "instructor." At the time, these descriptions both delighted and disturbed me. On the one hand, given my commitment to feminist pedagogy, I was glad to be perceived as a mediator. However, precisely because I am often read as "young," I worry about establishing a position of authority, especially among male students who sometimes question my right to be one. Because I was also beginning my first year as an assistant professor when Jeff wrote this essay, I was especially anxious about presenting a properly "professorial" persona. Was I wrong to tell my students they could call me "Julie" instead of "Dr. Jung"?

Jeff took this class with me during his first semester at the university. We were both new, both facing revisions in personal identity that scared and excited us. What does it mean to be a professor? How does one become a university student? And how does one achieve this sense of self and belong to the community it signifies when one is also unruly, willing and needing to question it, doubt it? Although the teacher in me felt threatened by Jeff's unruliness, another part of me identified with it. Instead of more strongly asserting my professorial authority over him that first semester, I decided to exploit the quality I perceived we shared: I praised his willingness to offer contrary interpretations. I encouraged him to write essays that challenged conventional forms. And I did so knowing full well his future English professors might not do the same.

In Jeff's narrative reflection, written two years after the essay quoted above, he comments on it as follows:

> In my first term at [the university], I wrote an interpretation of a book I used in Advanced Exposition class. I believe the instructor thought that I had a problem with the class; however, it was more of a personal discussion with myself while trying to figure out not only the selection of essays, but also what makes an essay good. As of now, I hope that the professor would be flattered to know that the paper was not a critique of the class, but rather an open expression where I felt comfortable to explain my confusion with the essay itself.

Here again he refers to me in third person, only now I am invoked as "instructor," as "professor." Furthermore, Jeff seeks to make amends with that professor, one he worries he may have previously insulted. He remarks that he felt "comfortable" explaining his confusion to me. As I reread this passage, I realize the unruliness—and our shared identity as unruly members of a university community— has disappeared.[10] While Jeff is clearly able to critique other authorities, I feel like he no longer trusts me to hear critiques of my class without punishing him with a bad grade. I'm nervous, wondering if I am no longer the open-minded thinker I once was, the teacher able and willing to create spaces for arguments that challenge her own.

And then I begin to understand why I let go unchallenged Jeff's contemptuous comment about his peers. In the two years between Advanced Composition and Senior Seminar, something changed. Jeff started calling me "Dr. Jung"; I started to like being called that. He started writing papers he did not believe in; I started to assign them. Somewhere along the line we found a way to belong. When Jeff told me that day in our empty classroom that he did not want to teach "these people," he rekindled within me a sense of myself I had not even realized I had been missing. Looking for the unruly one in both of us, I laughed. What saddens me is that I did not realize until now how domesticated my laughter has become. Making fun of students isn't unruly. I used to know that. But neither is defending them, especially in published scholarship where talking badly about one's students is virtually unheard of.

By rhetorically listening to my analysis of Jeff's essay, I am able to push beyond reflection as guilt-ridden self-critique. I can also move past the easy responses of defensive critique (of Jeff's comments) and unproblematized identification (of that version of me I first saw in Jeff's essay). Instead, I am finding a harder way to respond, one that forces me to locate my professorial identity within a discursive realm that both affirms and resists it. While I am comfortable resisting the conditions of my belonging, it is my desire to simultaneously affirm those very conditions that gives me pause. In this pause lies the possibility of revisionary consciousness.

Beyond RhetComp: Multigenre Tensions, Disciplinary Revisions

When rhetoric and composition teachers invite students to write in genres typically limited to literature and creative writing classes, they will inevitably confront resistance—from their students, their colleagues, their departments, themselves. In typical (and perhaps annoyingly upbeat) revisionary fashion, I advocate that we mine these resistances so that we might learn from them. In my particular case, studying Jeff's multigenre essay (and my reactions to it) has forced me to confront my assertion that I am beginning to assign essays I do not believe in. That sentence, which appears in the second-to-last paragraph of the previous section, surprises me, given that the purpose of this book is to advocate the usefulness of writing I *do* believe in. As I ponder why I made such a statement, I review the assignments I developed for Heather's and Jeff's class, the first of which was a close reading of a lengthy and complex essay.

And another Burkean metaphor rears its head.

Typically associated with out-of-date literature professors long overdue for retirement, close readings are obviously problematic for rhetoric teachers precisely because they are arhetorical. Such assignments, which practice New Critical theories by asking students to uncover textual meaning, are "wrong" because they ignore the rhetorical contexts within which writers write texts and readers interpret them. Presumably, I am ideologically opposed to them.

How could I have ever assigned such a beast?

To make matters worse, in other courses I have gone to great lengths to expose my students to the limitations of such readings. For example, in an undergraduate rhetorical theory course, I typically assign a work of short fiction and then ask students to write introductions to two different essays—a literary analysis and a rhetorical analysis. In an effort to help them make (dis)connections across the subfields of literature and RhetComp, I then ask them to reflect on the similarities and differences they observe in their two introductions. After reading and writing introductions to essays analyzing Alice Walker's short story, "Everyday Use," for example, one student, Laura, notes that in her literary analysis she focused on the story's "symbolism—always ever popular in literature!" By contrast, her rhetorical analysis considers the effects of "what is left unspoken." As Laura explains, "Rhetorically, you could ask, why are these things implied rather than stated outright?" Focusing on Walker's silences rather than her symbols, Laura questions Walker's decisions as a writer, pondering the degree to which her implied meanings and omitted contextual references enable her to accomplish her purpose. She wonders, for example, whether a given reader will know enough history to pick up on the story's irony. Laura's ability to consider the effectiveness of Walker's text within the context of a reader's interpretive repertoire stands in marked contrast to her simple and decontextualized interpretation of symbolic meaning.

Like Laura, most of my students respond to this assignment positively. They begin to realize they possess the skills necessary to interpret texts in different ways, and this realization feels empowering. However, when faced with the task of (re)interpreting nonfiction, my students fall apart. Although most of them, as English majors, have been reading stories, novels, and poems since elementary school, they have read very few complex nonfiction pieces, arguments that span over four pages and defy a simple thesis summary. Their lack of skill is, of course, tied to their lack of practice. Many of my students tell me they've never before been asked to read and respond to a lengthy nonfiction argument. Consequently, I am expecting too much if I think my students will be able to rhetorically analyze such texts before becoming familiar with their generic conventions.

In other words, I believe rhetoric teachers bear the particular burden of teaching students how to closely read nonfiction, and I expect this belief will cause me some trouble. First, if I start to assign close readings seriously, I will need to revise my favorite literary vs. rhetorical analysis assignment described above. More specifically, I can no longer be satisfied with an assignment that clearly sets up literature to be the fall guy; instead, I will have to distribute a nonfiction piece as well as a short story in order to more adequately assess my students' interpretive repertoire. Second, I will no longer be able to position old-timers in literature as my ignorant other; instead I will be forced to consider the merits of close readings and, by extension, the teachers who assign them. Finally, I will need to find effective ways to respond to my colleagues in rhetoric and composition studies, who will no doubt question my professional legitimacy when I finally muster the courage and admit to having a skeptical but insistent affinity for the close reading.

These insights into the tensions I construct and experience within and beyond RhetComp emerged only after analyzing my students' multigenre texts. By listening rhetorically to them, I am prompted not only to revise my attitudes toward the close reading and those who assign it, but also to ask: Why does the close reading remain for me the symbol of everything that is wrong with literature, even though I apparently find a lot right with it? An answer, of course, is that traditionally defined close readings are not supposed to "do" anything—they simply exist to explicate a text (usually a "great" one), and, when finished, the explication is considered complete rather than one piece of a more layered and complex analytical puzzle.

However, when I return to my students' texts, I realize that this answer, which again positions my rhetorical approach to literature as superior to those used by my colleagues in literature—is also in need of revision. That is, the one genre glaringly absent from all my students' texts was the traditionally defined close reading itself. Examples of literary analyses students *did* include instead reflect a "texts in contexts" approach, where students interpret literary texts by situating them within a variety of theoretical contexts, including Feminism, New Historicism, and Marxism. (Jeff's analysis of portrayals of the working class in Victorian literature is one such example.)

And so, it seems, many of my colleagues in literature, like me, are asking students to write beyond the close reading, to develop their skills in textual explication in order to construct more contextualized—dare I say, rhetorical?—readings. That said, I have no doubt that tensions do exist, and will continue to exist, between the "us" in RhetComp and the "them" in literature. Nevertheless, perhaps it is time some of us loosen our grip on the close reading and search for a new symbol, one that more productively identifies our most important differences.

4 / Toward Hearing the Impossible
A Multigenre Revision of Robert Connors's
"Teaching and Learning as a Man"—Revised

In chapters 2 and 3, I argue that one of the values of multigenre texts is their ability to force readers into a productive silence, one that both demands and offers fuller ways of listening. This productive silence is especially needed when scholars in rhetoric and composition studies are writing on issues constrained by existing disciplinary "slots," binary positionings that legitimize reductive readings and limit our resources for making knowledge. In this chapter, I analyze my own reductive reading of a well-known essay in the discipline, arguing that its traditional form failed to create a space for deeper listening.[1] I then revise the essay, recasting it in a multigenre, multivocal form. My purpose is to analyze how my revision facilitates deeper listening, thereby enabling me to construct knowledge that contributes to two ongoing debates in feminist composition: (1) What is feminist argument? and (2) What purpose, if any, does research on men serve in feminist composition scholarship?

I chose Robert Connors's "Teaching and Learning as a Man" because both the essay's content and my responses to it address the issues announced above. As will become apparent later in this chapter, my early readings of the essay did not expand my point of view. Instead, I opted to reach consensus with his argument by "agreeing to disagree": He thinks feminist composition scholars have ignored issues pertaining to male teachers and students; I think that charge is ridiculous, given the purpose of a subfield called *feminist* composition studies. By agreeing to disagree in this manner, I was able to remain steadfast in my original position, which kept me safely aligned with a feminist composition community with which I strongly wish to identify. But this reading, I realize, also failed to obligate me to listen in any way other than one that results in "easy" disagreement.

In an effort to delay consensus in meaning and gain new knowledge, I interviewed male writing teachers to learn about their experiences teaching male students. I offer the results of this research in the form of a multigenre, multivocal revision of Connors's essay, with the goal being to demonstrate how the multigenre version created spaces for me to contend with the silences in Connors's essay and my readings of it. I conclude with a revised response to Connors's essay, one informed by my new knowledge, which both critiques Connors's position as it affirms my investment in identifying with a feminist composition community from which I hesitate to separate myself. Specifically, I examine my resistance to feminist compositionists' calls for pedagogies that counter an "ethic of care" and advocate agonistic debate.

Before moving on, I would like to comment on my decision to continue with this argument, despite Robert Connors's untimely death in 2000. I do so because the issues he raised in his controversial article remain with us, and I am grateful to him for having had the courage to publish something he no doubt knew would make many people angry. Some might say that I should honor Robert Connors's memory and analyze my responses to something else. I disagree. I think continuing to work with and against his research testifies to its importance. As scholars and academics, we honor each other in no better way.

Arguing about Feminist Argument

For me, one of the most interesting debates in current feminist composition scholarship contends with the form and function of argument. Many feminist compositionists are dissatisfied with early formulations of feminist argument, which advocate compromise and consensus-building without considering the contexts within which such agreements are forged. Susan Jarratt ("Case"), for example, has persuasively argued that social hierarchies remain within even the most feminist classrooms, and the power differentials that exist among students should lead us to question the merits of "compromise" and "consensus," positive terms that no doubt obscure the problematics of surrender. Rather than rely on pedagogies that smooth over conflict, Jarratt advocates strategies that help students engage productively with conflicts as they argue about public issues. Given their commitment to eradicating oppressive structures and practices, it would seem that feminist compositionists would enthusiastically embrace Jarratt's call. Their resistance to doing so Jarratt locates within a pedagogical context that privileges expressivist theories and an "ethic of care," where teachers try to create safe and nurturing spaces for students to give voice to their authentic selves. For many feminist teachers, such a pedagogy remains appealing, as it authorizes those who have been and continue to be silenced to speak. Furthermore, it does so while also steering clear of agonistic debates that can disrupt students' feelings of safety and comfort.

Despite these strong appeals, Jarratt and others warn us that expressivism creates more problems than it solves. First, as Jarratt explains, expressivist pedagogies reinforce the troubling metaphor of writing teacher as nurturing mother, which, when deployed within a feminized field well known for its exploitative labor practices and perception as "women's work," validates the very logic feminist compositionists argue against. Second, in an intellectual age that questions claims to a stable self and an authentic voice, expressivism fails to offer a sophisticated theory for engaging with conflict and difference. In other words, if our only goal is to express our authentic voices, how do we learn to listen and respond to the voices of others? And what are we to make of the fact that our "authentic" voices change, depending on the contexts within which we speak?

Given the limitations of expressivism, recent compositionists have sought to use the power of the "coming to voice" metaphor within formulations of argument that avoid expressivist foundations. Jarratt, for example, discusses the potential of arguments that situate personal experiences within specific social and historical contexts. Nedra Reynolds ("Interrupting") advocates a concept of agency that enables a speaker to both find a voice and then use it to interrupt and intervene in the oppressive discourses encountered in everyday life. Lynch, George, and Cooper theorize argument as "confrontational cooperation," which "includes both confrontational and cooperative perspectives, a multifaceted process that includes moments of conflict and agonistic positioning as well as moments of understanding and communication" (63). By recognizing the historical and cultural contingencies of subjectivity, these scholars offer sophisticated theories of argument that advocate the rhetorical usefulness of productive discomfort, and they do so without reproducing the masculinist metaphor of argument as war.

Arguing about Men

A second debate that interests me is whether feminist composition scholars are obligated to research issues involving men and masculinity. Although performative gender theories question the usefulness of even constructing such a debate, it nevertheless exists, and my immediate response to it as a feminist has always been "of course not." Then Robert Connors published his essay, and I found myself needing to offer a more sophisticated reply. However, as we often hope happens with our students, in the process of forming my reply, I began to question it. Furthermore, I began to question the forms I was using to communicate that reply. In other words, as someone interested in forging arguments that do not reproduce masculinist metaphors of argument as war, I observed with some irony that my responses were indeed quite warlike. Witness the following opening of an early rough draft:

> In "Teaching and Learning as a Man," Robert Connors ticks me off, makes me angry, begs me to demolish his argument with an avalanche of logical, articulate, indisputable counterattacks.

Of course, I quickly realized that I couldn't actually say that in an academic article, so I sought out other people's critiques, hoping I could diffuse my anger by couching it in appropriately scholarly practices of citation.

In "Male Flight and Feminist Threat in Composition Studies," Laura Micciche critiques Connors's essay in three ways. First, she exposes the reductive quality of his cause/effect historical analysis, which locates men's confusion within a single origin that fails to contextualize the political, economic, and social forces involved in women's entrance into the academy and the feminization of composition. Second, she challenges his ethos as both historian and feminist supporter by noting his refusal to foreground his own interpretive investment and his failure to cite more feminist research. Third, she charges that his thinking is weak because it is founded on troubling binaries regarding the roles men and women should assume in liberatory work. Furthermore, according to Miccichie, Connors's assertions reveal unproblematized and depoliticized assumptions about the writing teacher's role as father, one where a nurturing parent tries to help his (male) children achieve self-actualization.

While Micciche most definitely lent quality ammunition in the battle to destroy Connors's argument, I was still dissatisfied. I wanted more of my initial anger to come through. I wanted people in the field to understand how offensive Connors's argument was to me, and not only because of the reasons explained above. So, I tried again.

As a feminist, I have trouble hearing Connors's argument for a number of reasons. First, by blaming feminism for men's confusion, he risks positioning himself as an "abandoned male," not the most rhetorically persuasive strategy given, as his description would have us believe, his audience of powerful feminists/pro-feminist intellectuals. His complaints that feminist writers fail to address him as a man—their failure to appeal to him personally—undermine his self-professed support of feminist goals. That is, if he truly understood feminist ideology, wouldn't he be able to do a better job of theorizing his exclusion?

And I'm not at all convinced that feminists in the academy and, more specifically, in rhetoric and composition studies, wield the kind of power Connors thinks we do. Despite the general lip service paid to feminist ideologies within academic circles, feminist academics still struggle in their attempts to challenge and revise hegemonic institutional beliefs and practices. As Gesa Kirsch's research (*Women*) compellingly illuminates, feminist scholars experience difficulty establishing their authority *as academics* because their work shakes the foundations upon which that authority is traditionally built. Specifically, Kirsch reports that scholars whose work disrupts traditional notions of "good" scholarship have a harder time getting published and more difficulty finding reviewers who are familiar with their cross-disciplinary work. The connection between getting published and holding real power within the academy is an obvious one, and yet Connors overlooks it. By failing to consider the research of scholars like Kirsch, Connors conveniently sidesteps the academy's present-day resistance to feminism.

While Kirsch's work demands that we reevaluate the success of feminism within a larger institutional context, Theresa Enos's research invites us to focus on women within rhetoric and composition studies in particular. More specifically, her work challenges Connors's implied assertion that women have got all—or most of—the power in this discipline. (By the way, I don't want to make the same mistake Connors makes and conflate "woman" and "feminist." A womanly presence is, of course, not a necessarily feminist one. Yet documenting women's struggles to access power in this discipline is an important first step, for it enables us to imagine the even greater struggles of self-identified and practicing feminists.)

If Connors is the advocate of feminism that he says he is, and I have my doubts, then I respond to his feelings of exclusion, his lack of social support, by telling him to educate other men about how they can become men in ways that don't oppress women, people of color, gays and lesbians. Despite his supposed support of the feminist project, Connors undermines it by creating a feminist/man binary that, in the end, simply serves to reinforce patriarchy. To get out from under the binary, Connors needs to articulate a men's movement that doesn't depend on its exclusion from feminism, but rather acts as a separate and necessary complement. In short, I would encourage Connors to foster connections with men so that together we might undermine patriarchy, not feminism.

To be sure, I felt better after writing the above, and I was confident in my ability to remove the name-calling and thereby make myself look like a more congenial member of the profession. And, after reading Gesa Kirsch's published "Comment" and observing the similarities between our responses (in terms of both tone and content), I was comforted by the knowledge that my anger was justified. Shortly thereafter, however, I remembered something Nancy Welch said in response to an analysis that appeared in her first academic publication:

> . . .[S]et up this authority, set up that, then tear them down, get on with what you want to say. I was shaken when, one year later, I met one of those authorities face to face. It occurred to me then, and should have occurred to me before, that she was more than a few words on the page I chose to quote: a living breathing person leading a complex life, asking complex questions—who she is and what her work is far exceeding the boundaries I'd drawn. (*Getting*, 147)

I never met Robert Connors. I used to read his postings on the WPA listserv, and sometimes I would think about emailing him, telling him about my research. I never did, though. It was easier that way.

As I mentioned earlier, a theory of argument as confrontational cooperation requires both agonistic positioning as well as understanding (Lynch et al., 63). As the above responses make clear, many of my feminist colleagues and I are well practiced in the art of agonistic debate. In fact, our success in academia is no doubt tied to our ability to engage in and win such debates. However, I am less skilled in attempting to understand the positions of those with whom I vehemently disagree, and I am not convinced that understanding should always be my goal. That is, in a social context where women are constructed "to yield, concede, make nice, smooth egos, avoid friction, take on the emotional work" (Greenbaum, 159), where "it has always been women's work to understand others" (Lamb, 17), I am reluctant to understand a position that threatens to reinscribe the very thinking my feminist politics seeks to disrupt.

Yet, what am I to make of my contradictory goals here? Connors's argument has clearly disrupted my comfortable worldview regarding the purpose and domain of feminist composition. Given my stated commitment to revisionary rhetoric, which seeks to explore these disruptions rather than shut them down (which I believe is what my earlier responses do in fact do), I should be willing to understand his position so that I might learn more about the roots of our conflict. What does it mean that I nearly abandon that commitment when faced with an argument that I do not like?

When I decided to theorize revision as a process of delayed convergence, one of staying with rather than deleting passages and texts that upset me, I made a commitment to myself and to my profession. I also made things much more difficult.

A Revisionary Rhetorician Tries Again

> Our ethnographic encounters have suggested in several
> different ways that a focus on unequal power, while essential
> in an ongoing way, is not a sufficient lens through which to
> explore our relation to "others," most particularly in an age
> when feminism and postmodernism also call for alliance, and
> alliance specifically across old relations of unequal power.
> —Judith Newton and Judith Stacey, "Ms.Representations:
> Reflections on Studying Academic Men"

In "Teaching and Learning as a Man," Robert Connors contends that in a discipline concerned with teaching, scholars must approach gender issues wholly. Because I agree, I am motivated to revise Connors's essay so that I and other feminist compositionists might be more persuaded to listen to it. His essay is ripe for revision because in it he uses a trope familiar to many feminist writers: exclusion. More specifically, he argues that as a man there is no serious place for him to discuss issues that affect men directly within a disciplinary context where feminists wield "increasingly real scholarly and institutional power" (142). Before revising Connors's essay in an effort to hear that which has been excluded, I will first describe feminist writing strategies that facilitate revisionary rhetoric.

In *The Disobedient Writer: Women and Narrative Tradition*, Nancy Walker analyzes the rhetorical strategies of women writers who seek to revise a literary tradition from which they have been excluded. She examines how women writers revise particular kinds of fictional and traditional texts—Bible stories, fairy tales, and canonical texts, such as *The Scarlet Letter*—that establish and legitimize a dominant cultural tradition. Women writers choose to revise these widespread, "public domain" stories in such a way as to expose patriarchal assumptions in the original. Their versions offer a kind of intertextuality that resees the word/world and examines the connections between original and revision, patriarchy and feminist theory.

Walker's central argument is that revisionary, feminist writing—what she terms "disobedient" writing—differs from common textual appropriation because the feminist writer's motives differ:

> Because of the way in which Western literary traditions have been formulated, . . . most male writers who have appropriated and revised previous texts have worked within a tradition that included them and their experience, whereas women writers have more commonly addressed such texts from the position of outsider, altering them either to point up the biases they encode or to make them into narratives that women can more comfortably inhabit. (3)

Rather then endorse the values of the dominant culture by continuing its narrative, a disobedient writer seeks to "expose or upset paradigms of authority inherent in the texts they appropriate" (7).

Walker's analyses of feminist texts are helpful because they outline key features of revisionary rhetoric. One such feature is the move to retell a "public domain" story, what we sometimes think of as history, through the lens of a previously peripheral or marginal point of view. By conferring agency to this slighted point of view, a revisionary rhetor is able to do two things. First, in making connections between revised and original texts, she exposes the constructed nature of all texts. She positions her story not as *the* story but instead as one among many. Second, by revealing the constructed nature of texts, she disrupts patriarchal notions of universality. Rather than hold her story up as Truth, the writer's self-conscious awareness of it as a revision of a prior text engages the reader, prompting him to question to "truth" validity of all texts. In a feminist, postmodernist context, these two rhetorical strategies are persuasive because they communicate to the reader the writer's knowledge of history as always partial and situated.

Furthermore, in the revised version, the previously marginalized character is now granted authority as speaker and is therefore capable of questioning and challenging the very forces that oppress her. As Walker explains, the speaker is

> enmeshed in a culture whose values denigrate her, and yet [she is able] to stand apart intellectually and comment on her own situation with an emotional detachment expressed as wit. This double consciousness is the narrative analogue to the process of revision: the character is both within history and outside of it, feeling the force of the moment and at the same time exercising a rhetorical freedom from it. (163)

By granting story-telling agency to a previously marginalized point of view, the revisionary rhetor creates a space for ironic commentary: The narrator exists in culture in such a way that she can experience it *and* critique it at the same time.

This ironic, double space is another important feature of revisionary rhetoric, for not only does it demand that readers see at least two versions of truth, but it also forges a bond between writer and reader and thus disrupts a writer/reader binary. Citing Wayne Booth, Walker explains this bond as follows:

> [T]he ironist presents statements that the reader recognizes as being untrue, and the reader, rejecting these statements, must then determine what the author's real meaning is and mentally reconstruct a statement that more nearly conforms to this meaning. (155)

Irony creates a bond between writer and reader because they are both "in on it," so to speak. And, because the writer's/character's point of view is not obvious, the reader shares some of the responsibility for making meaning. Thus, the writer's creation of an ironic double perspective creates readerly work: rereading, reconstructing, revising. The reader is forced to ask, "What is true here?" The question itself demands that she recognize the existence of other possibilities and construct for herself the best meaning in a particular context; it reveals the situatedness of the reader's own knowledge-making, which opens spaces for other situations, other points of view.

Connors himself uses this kind of ironic double perspective at the start of his essay, and it is what creates an initial bond between us. Describing his experiences conferencing with one "burley" male student who came to his office for help, Connors writes:

> When he had gotten as thorough a set of marching orders as he could draw from me—and I, young prof, was happy to dispense my gems of wisdom in good detail to those astute enough to ask for them—he departed quickly and with relief. (137)

Mocking himself and out-of-date pedagogies that hold the teacher as knowledge-disseminator, Connors wins me over. "Marching orders," "gems of wisdom," "those astute enough to ask for them." I see the two of us, drinking coffee, an eyebrow raised, maybe one of us is laughing. We're remembering those early days, how much smarter than our students we thought we were, how much we didn't know about teaching and conferencing and journaling. We can laugh now, of course, because those days are behind us.

Or are they? For me, Connors's description wins me over because some of what he says still holds true. I still feel proud and pleased when students ask me for my "gems of wisdom." I walk out of the office, my head a little higher than usual. I feel useful, like I have something to offer and someone willing and ready to receive. Connors helps me poke fun at myself, but there is also an edge in his words. In his description of the young prof, I see a hard truth about—one version of—myself: I am a do-gooder with a big ego and pedantic tendencies that border on the hegemonic. His irony shows me that I am "in on it" in more ways than one.

The initial bond I feel with Connors—we're both teachers capable of critiquing the academic culture that creates us—is severed, of course, when he locates his anger toward his student within a larger context of feeling insecure about how to relate to this male student, which, as I have discussed earlier, he locates within a still larger context of feminism's influence in the academy. He could keep me as a reader and make me take a hard look at the contradictions, the stereotypes, the problems that exist within feminist pedagogy if he began by making clear the tradition from which he feels excluded. Part of that tradition, of course, is evident from his works cited page: the Belenky et al. and Gilligan "Women Ways" tradition, which in its day revised prevailing male-centered theories of epistemological and moral development. As we know, *Women's Ways of Knowing* and *In a Different Voice* are themselves feminist revisions of the sort analyzed by Walker: They rewrite and revise disciplinary narratives by retelling the story from a previously marginalized point of view—women. Less obviously, Connors's title—"Teaching and Learning *as a* Man" (emphasis added)—refers to Elizabeth Flynn's often cited and influential "Composing as a Woman," an essay that begins with Adrienne Rich's famous call to revise "men's thinking." Like Connors, Flynn explores linkages between composition studies and feminist theory. Like Connors, she cites *Women's Ways of Knowing* and *In a Different Voice*, arguing for revised writing pedagogies that recognize women's different epistemological and moral locations, an argument that, like Connors's, rests on uncomfortable generalities regarding male students' preferences for separation and individuation, and female students' desire for connection and relationship. Thus, we find Connors in the difficult position of wanting to retell a recently retold story. That is, the tradition from which Connors feels excluded is a quintessentially feminist *tradition of revision*.

For Connors to enter this tradition, *to fit in by not fitting in,* he would need to embark on a disobedient reading of the "Women's Ways" tradition. In other words, he must retell that tradition from a marginal and previously unheard point of view in such a way as to "expose or upset the paradigms of authority inherent in the texts" he appropriates (Walker, 7). Furthermore, his task is all the more difficult because he must rewrite the prevailing tradition without returning to patriarchal foundations that the first retellings sought to disrupt. That is, he can hardly enter a feminist tradition by making patriarchal claims. Unfortunately, this is exactly what he ends up of doing, as I discuss earlier. Rather than abandon Connors precisely when he needs me most, I choose to cling to that sliver of connection and ask: *Who is being excluded here?* Whose voice has yet to be heard? Surely we have heard Robert Connors—rhetoric and composition scholar, well-known and respected historian. In fact, we hear this version of Robert Connors in the bulk of his essay. But on page 149, someone else steps in, briefly but powerfully:

> If, like many of us, you were a nerdy kid picked on by the tough guys, dealing from a position of (provisional) power with their contemporary incarnations is a relationship filled with unspeakable issues.

Connors is referring to problems male teachers can have connecting with certain types of "burley" and "aggressive" male students who challenge them in outdated but nevertheless omnipresent agonistic ways. What interests me more here is not the content of Connors's point so much as the emergence of this nerdy kid from the shadows, the one who was picked on, the one who goes silent in the face of those unspeakable issues. Who is he? What was school like for *him*? How did he cope? As a feminist, I hear "unspeakable issues" and I turn an ear toward keener listening. My mind races, wanting to get to know him, wanting to hear his story, realizing that knowing *his* story might help me help my male students to write.

But I do not get to hear his story, the very point of view that might disrupt prevailing assumptions and help us to understand male students' emotional silences and "inexpressivity" more fully. Indeed the one thing about which Connors is virtually silent—save the reference to the nerdy kid—is his own schooling experiences, his own struggles overcoming emotional constriction. In short, the one thing that could save Connors would be for him to live up to the implications of his title: What does it *feel* like to teach and learn as a man?

"Teaching and Learning as a Man": A Multigenre, Multivocal Revision

In the spring of 1997, when I first read Connors's essay, I responded with an immediate and intense anger, the kind of visceral reaction that makes scholars nervous but which can be mined to yield potentially transformative knowledge. To help me arrive at this knowledge, to produce what Jane E. Hindman calls "embodied writing," I decided to interview my male colleagues to hear how they understood his argument and what reactions, if any, they had to it. I wrote a memo and distributed it to all of the male graduate teaching assistants who teach writing at the University of Arizona.[2] Eleven of my colleagues, all of them white males in their mid-twenties to early forties, agreed to read Connors's essay and then be interviewed. I met with each of them for approximately one and one-half to two hours. We met at coffee shops around Tucson, in the Student Union Mexican restaurant, in the graduate student lounge, at my apartment. We talked about teaching, mentoring, poetry, friendship, life. While excerpts of these interviews are not intended to convey any statistical significance, they did help me begin to understand what my male colleagues experience as writing teachers and learners. As such, I offer their insights to my readers in much the same way. Through their words, I hope to give voice to the silences in Connors's essay.

Separating

When asked whether they consider themselves mentors to their male students, many of the interviewees described practical limitations that keep them from taking on such a role. Ryan, a 32-year-old experienced teacher, situates his hesitation within an increasingly litigious context that makes blurred relationships with students problematic:

> When I knew I wanted to become a teacher, I started tutoring at an elementary school and one of the hard and fast rules—it was a law—was never to be alone with a student in a classroom ever. It didn't matter if you knew this student well or not. I think I've grown up in terms of teaching in this culture with a "don't get too close" attitude, because it can open up all sorts of weird legal problems. I've never had a problem with a student that's developed into anything serious, thank god. I'm sure I'll have them down the line, and I'll have to deal with them. But I've had plenty of friends who've had students who've been no end of trouble. Calling in the parents. Doing the grade review process. Threatening to sue. All that stuff. So, yeah, I'd like to be a mentor to any student who'd like me to be a mentor, but at the same time I think I draw back from that, to a large degree. Some of my male friends who are teachers are very comfortable with telling students, "I don't want to talk to you in this capacity. I don't want to be your friend," etc. I have more trouble with that. I see myself as an advocate for students, as a student's friend. Maybe that's good, maybe that's bad. I haven't decided yet. I don't know. But I naturally fall into very comfortable relationships with

students, both male and female. I think it's a good thing, but I don't know. The jury's still out on that one.

Like Ryan, other interviewees expressed an interest in developing mentoring relationships with their students but noted that time limitations and their own work demands make such relationships difficult. For example, as John, 33, explains:

> I don't have time, unfortunately, to be too many people's mentors. And I feel like I choose people who can most benefit from it and who need it and who have the most potential. Like that Josh kid. I am his mentor. I am. He was in my 102 class, my 209 class, I get together with him, he declared himself a creative writing major because of me. He's got so much talent and so much potential. In any way, if I can help him out, I will, in any way that I can. I read his stuff. He's very respectful of my boundaries. I mean, we're friends.

Tony, 28, who describes himself as an "isolationist," expresses a similar concern about students' need to recognize his boundaries:

> Is this somebody who, when I see him, I want to dive behind the garbage can so I don't have to be "on"? I feel like I always have to be "on" when I go to campus. I'm like, "I'm not 'on,' okay? I just want to get my fucking mail and get out of here."

In addition, Tony is concerned about the responsibility of mentoring, which he describes as something he's "uneasy about" because he worries that his male students will think he's gay:

> I have this paranoia that if I'm getting too close to a male student, he's going to think I'm gay, think I'm interested. I'm uncomfortable with those boundaries. They're unfamiliar to me, not the sexual ones, but the teacher-student relationship.

Several other teachers located their struggles to mentor male students within a social context where homophobia is the norm. For example, when I asked John how men might work together to develop a brotherhood that doesn't depend on violence, like those bonds that form in many fraternities and on all-male sports teams, he responded, "There's probably an element of homophobia that prohibits that from taking off more." Working against Connors's depiction of sports as a form of male bonding too dependent on violence, Paul explains:

> There's a way that Connors talks about Men's Studies that sounds intelligent to me; it sounds like it could have interesting results, or bring up interesting stuff. The Men's Movement has been made to sound really silly, and I think it's worth questioning why. There's a place for hugging trees, there really is. But if it's written into a program, I'm suspicious of it. I like the idea of men bonding and communicating. But I'm suspicious of programs. Playing basketball is something you know I do a lot. I get something out of that, even if it's veiled, even if it's cloaked, even if the homosocial sexual stuff is metaphorized into this game, you're still doing it, you're still rubbing bodies, you're still getting physical. And that's happening. That is happening. And you get something out of it.

Some interviewees situated their hesitancy to mentor male students within a professional context, one where the job of a writing teacher is to teach writing rather than to mentor male students:

> This self-consciousness about becoming a role model is a problem. In situations where you've had positive relationships with professors, doesn't that stem from an academic relationship first, a certain kind of interest that's shared, or an enthusiasm that you have for something? Five-sixths of the kids in these classes couldn't give a crap about what you're talking about. So this idea of manufacturing an

avenue for us to send out touchy-feely feelers to these students . . . I wonder how valuable that is. Aren't your students more apt to be attracted to you if you actually taught
them something? Or is it the content of the class that can
lead to that bridge? Working mentoring into the curriculum seems like a weird thing to do. Maybe I'm being too
hard on the guy [Connors].—Todd, 25.

Some of the interviewees also revealed how their own past relationships with men, particularly their fathers, inhibit their desire
to form close relationships with other men. As John explains:

I haven't spoken to my own father in thirteen years and I
don't like older men because of that and I don't trust anybody. I don't like to get too involved with people on that
level. So, I'm aware of it as a problem, and then reading this
[Connors's] essay made me realize that it's a problem for a
lot of men. And then it makes me think about when I was
even younger, when I was [an undergraduate] and I didn't
want to listen to anybody. [Lists undergraduate creative
writing teachers] All those guys were failures to me. They
were writers who had to teach. Failures. I did not respect
them for that reason, and that was wrong. So wrong. It
colored everything, my whole education was colored, ru-
ined, essentially, by that misperception.

Tony, who describes his own relationship with his father as "lacking," explains how his father's absence led him to develop destruc-
tive relationships with men:

Growing up, I was always looking for some male presence.
I found it in these guys that my sisters were dating, and I
think it was kind of dangerous in a lot of ways, the triangles
that were set up. Later it came through sports. Definitely
that's the way violence is institutionalized. I played football in college and doing the sickest, craziest, most violent

things was rewarded. We'd get in fights and break things, all that kind of stuff. It had merit in that world.

Scott, 40, doesn't mention his father when asked about male mentor figures, but his struggle to explain the absence of influential male figures in his life is apparent in his response:

> I don't like men much. It's tough to put into words, this part of it. I think . . . let me think for a second. I've sought out . . . [silence] I don't know what it is. I really don't know what it is. I'll have to think about it. [silence] This could just be an individual thing, but when I think back to the women advisors I had . . . mentors . . . who seemed just truly interested, seemed to have good solid concern about my progress. With the few male professors I've had it almost seemed like a check-list: "Okay, what are you taking? Okay, great." I don't know if that's purely just individual coincidence or if there's something there. I don't know. But I've never really felt the kind of connection with male professors that I've had with women professors. After nailing Connors for making sweeping generalizations, I hesitate to do the same thing, but it's my experience. I don't know. The professors I keep in touch with are women professors, two or three. I still communicate with them. There's no sense of urgency to keep in touch with the guys. I don't know what it is.

While describing healthy relationships with fathers and former male teachers, several of the interviewees explained how these relationships have been and continue to be both rewarding and problematic. As Paul, 30, relates:

> My father is a troubling mentor, but I thank god for him. I fear what I would be had my mother been the only one at my helm because she was so neglectful. He wasn't there completely, and he wasn't completely my father, but I've

grown under his wing, and I'm glad. He got me into school. He helped me get through junior college and then transferring to college. So he's a real source of strength for me. [What's he like?] He's very judgmental, and that can be a hard thing to live with. I can be very judgmental, but I fight more for a compassionate side. His judgment has been a burden and at times has been a difficult thing to live under. Everything I used to read I wanted to show him, "Look! Look. Look at this. Here's where you're contradicted." I wanted to show him James Baldwin. But I don't feel that so much anymore. I'm not so much under his wing. He's also been encouraging to me. It used to be we had clashes. One of the best things he said to me when he came [to visit] the other day, and I didn't ask him to say this, but he said, "You should be an essayist. You have these ideas." I wrote him a letter a couple of summers ago when I drove from Louisville to Arkansas and I wrote him about it and he's like, "This is a good piece of writing." He was really impressed with it. And he started to say that I could be a writer, which has always been a trouble spot for me. He's a writer. A successful writer. He writes. And he's written some good things, has written a lot of trash, but it's writing. Made a million bucks in one year.

I decided to interview my colleagues and revise Connors's essay because my emotional response to it told me it was saying something I needed to hear. At first I thought that something was pretty simple: Men aren't the only ones who prefer separation. Before reading Connors's essay, I'd never even thought of myself as a mentor to my female students. Growing up, I used to spend long, isolated hours in my parents' bedroom, leafing through old family photographs, looking for something I needed but didn't know how to find.

Connecting

While many of the interviewees' responses support claims that men prefer separation over connection and relatedness, especially when

connections thwart individual achievement, other responses contradict these claims. For example, while several of the interviewees
described the absence of male mentor figures in their early lives, they
also revealed their desire for them. As Paul explains, "Of course I
wanted a mentor. I *yearned* for male guidance to show me the way.
And I guess also to be there when I was depressed and to recognize
my unhappiness." John echoes Paul's desire: "I needed [a male men-
tor] so bad. I was in a great deal of pain—as a lot of young men are—
that I often could not see out of. No one jarred me out of it at all."

For many of the interviewees, their own past disconnections
with older men serve as springboards for fostering connections with
younger men. John, for example, whose own troubled relationship
with his father caused him to distrust male mentor figures, reflects
on how this history enables him to connect with male students who
seem to distrust him:

> I have guys in my classes who are just like me. And I know
> how to break through to those people. I got a couple of
> emails from [a male student] asking if he could just hang
> out with me for a little bit, just to continue to vibe off of
> me. And he said, "I walked into this classroom thinking
> that this was going to be a disaster. It was a requirement
> and I did not want to have to take this class. I wanted to
> skip right to [advanced poetry writing]." I know how to
> deal with that kind of character because I was that kind of
> character, who didn't want to listen to anybody.

John later describes how this same student's troubled relationship
with his father sparked an emotional breakthrough that deepened
their connection:

> After a 102 class one day Josh and I were hanging around
> and he just all of a sudden broke down crying because his
> father had tried to borrow money from him. And he's like
> a scholarship dorm kid, barely making it, sells lemonade
> at baseball games to make a little money. Here his father is

trying to borrow a 100 bucks. He doesn't need that. It was just too much pressure for him. And at that point it was kind of like at that moment I was jarred into thinking, "I could do some good here" and I had already jarred him into thinking, "Okay, this is somebody I maybe need to get to know a little better." I think he had the same problem [as I did when I was a first-year student]. He's in a lot of pain—intellectual and emotional pain—but he saw his way out a little bit. He could see out of his own head enough to seek out help.

Similarly, Ryan describes how his own rebellious streak as a student in high school enables him to connect with and respond positively to male students who challenge his authority:

I used to do it. And students try to do it to me. They know this will piss Teacher X off. Teacher X has expressed certain ideas about the world, and this student is now going to show them that they don't give a shit. In high school I wrote those kind of essays all the time, especially with teachers you didn't like and who you thought were looking at you unfairly. I can definitely remember essays I've written that were intended to piss the teacher off. That was my goal.

I get very confrontational, very agonistic male students all the time, students who are willing to call me on anything that I say that suggests to them that they should do something about their writing or that they have something to learn. My approach is . . . [laughter] I always think of the old *Kung Fu* TV series. There was this one moment when his teacher said, "You must bend like the willow." I bend. I don't let male students who are confrontational phase me, because all my life I've grown up with guys like that, and when you're confrontational, that's what they want. It buys right into their ploy. If you bend, all of the sudden they realize there's less to rebel against. That's a lesson I had to learn in my life.

Scott also describes strategies he uses to connect with confrontational male students who attempt to disconnect with him and his course:

> There's an anxiety in the classroom, definitely, that has to do with male teachers and young men. I'm challenged all the time on the testosterone level . . ."poetry is for fags" . . . "why are we reading this?" . . . that sort of thing. What do you do about those guys in their baseball caps? I let them know from the get-go that I'm a student, too. I'm not here to deliver wisdom. I tell most of them on the first day of class, "If you're looking for that kind of advice, quit school right now, learn how to surf, spend a year in France or Africa, come back and dedicate a year of your life to charity, spend 30 or 60 days in a county jail, get your heart broken a few times, then come to college. It makes much more sense." That's just to let them know. "But since we're here let's [laughter] read some poems." I position myself both intellectually and even right there in the classroom configuration physically as more of a student. And it seems to work.

Scott later describes one particularly difficult male student with whom he was eventually able to connect:

> I had a fellow for two semesters. He was just the most violently obnoxious person I'd ever met. He absolutely undermined everything I did, both in the class and on the listserv. He refused to budge. He dressed in all black. I swear to god he was a crack smoker. He's sort of a lunatic. He was an asshole in class, an asshole on the listserv. But when he came to office hours or if we passed each other on campus [he was] the nicest guy in the world. And I used to ask him, "What is your deal?! Why are you nice to me here? Why can we talk here but not in class?" He would just shrug it off. At the beginning of the second semester, he told me, "I'm intimidated by all of this. In high school I was the tough guy. I got all the girls. I owned three electric guitars,

a car. I come here and everybody's cooler than I am." So he
was lashing out. Lashing out at me because I like poetry, the
evil thing. And I still get emails from him to this day. He quit
his fraternity. He realized that wasn't for him. That's someone . . . I would never put this on my teaching self-evaluation . . . he was someone who needed to be told to grow up.
Whether you're supposed to do that in a writing class, I
don't know. I don't know. But he took his writing seriously,
more seriously, after we had talked. Before it was just taunt-
ing: "I think this. What are you going to do about it?"

In addition to connecting with confrontational students who
reminded them of themselves at that age, several of the interviewees
described other kinds of relationships with male students, connections spurred by mutual admiration or loneliness. Ryan, for example, who earlier explained how our litigious culture prevents him
from fostering mentoring relationships with students, works against
this formulation when he says:

When it comes to teaching I'm always pushing for more
human relationships, even though they're messy, even
though they're complex. I shy away from these kind of
administrative formulas for teacher-student relationships,
like "Never be alone with a student in classroom." They
seem so anti-human to me. Sure, we're screwed up people,
but we're trying to do something about it rather than develop laws to isolate us from each other.

He later describes one such relationship with a male student, a relationship founded on shared admiration for two famous poets:

One male student who I've had coffee with and who I've kept
in touch with ever since class ended—he's a fascinating
guy—he decided to go visit William Burroughs and Allen
Ginzberg. He called up William Burroughs and said, "Can I
live with you over the summer?" This was like three years

ago, when he was still in high school, and William Burroughs
said, "yes," so he went and lived with the guy for six weeks.
He brought all these pictures in. It was like, "oh my god!"
He was fascinating. We struck up a relationship after class.
We had coffee and we continue to, once every four months
or so, something like that. He'll ask me about course work,
about what courses are good to take, what's this major like,
what should I do with my life, that type of stuff.

Tony, who earlier described himself as an "isolationist," someone
who feels uncomfortable with mentoring because of the intimacy
it requires, later powerfully presents himself as a caring and competent mentor:

The first person who came to my office hours came to talk
to me about his first paper. He sounded very confused, reluctant to even talk about it. He was very shy. I had a big
chew of tobacco in my mouth, and it took 15 minutes for
me to realize that he was coming to me because he was
lonely. He's from Minnesota and felt totally out of place, had
no friends, and was really just reaching out to me. It really
hit me. I was like, "wow." It touched me, and it also alarmed
me to the responsibilities I had. Here's this jackass chew-
ing tobacco. What kind of impression am I setting for him?
Halfway through the conversation I realized that he was there
for other reasons, and I tried to reach out for him and I felt
sort of surprised by the weight of the responsibility. It was
the first time I'd ever been in that position in my life. I think
at that point I tried to talk to him about other stuff. What
was going on? What about home? What did he miss about
home? I think he left feeling better about things. But from
then on he'd be in almost every week. I started giving him
books and we had this little book club. He was into it.
  He wrote some really powerful things. His personal ex-
ploratory essay was about his father abusing him basically.
He'd spent the first 17 years of his life in one place and then

he moved between junior and senior year in high school and was really traumatized by that. He also had a pretty troubled relationship with his father. So it was about conflicts between him and his father and how his older brother was the intermediary who was living outside of the house. He'd go to his brother's house anytime shit hit the fan at his house. His father would hit him, throw him around. That's what was in the essay. He has an incredible voice, a really natural voice as a writer. I encouraged him to write.

Before I even picked up and read Carol Gilligan's *In a Different Voice*, I had her argument reduced to a set of easily remembered binaries: women—connection, relationship (read: emotion); men—separation, achievement (read: inexpressivity). Then I actually read her book, and I realized quickly that I was doing her research a disservice by representing the concept of relationship in such simplified terms. In the closing paragraph of her chapter titled, "Images of Relationship," Gilligan disrupts the commonplace that relationship equals connection when she describes the "paradoxical truths of human experience—"

> that we know ourselves as separate only insofar as we live in connection with others, and that we experience relationship only insofar as we differentiate other from self. (63)

Connection and separation. Other and self. Love and pain. These are the paradoxes of relationship, and only by recognizing their manifestation in *all* relationships, from collaborative groups consisting of women only to male mentorships between writing teacher and student, only then can we begin to address human issues wholly.

Separating
John:

> Men are walking around in academia like they've got a target on their back. On egg shells a little bit. And maybe we

should. Stephen Dunn the poet said—I'm paraphrasing—there's a problem when one gender has earned the right to complain, and we will all be better off when that situation is righted. And is that fair to say, that one sex has in fact earned to right to complain? Like, feminists in academia—I'm not the enemy. I'm trying to understand, at least. If they want to find a real enemy, go out to the monster truck crap and wrestling matches and the dog races and the horse races and the fraternities and football. If there's any enemy, that's the enemy. But they don't want to talk to those people. They want to browbeat me because I'm of the same sex as those other idiots. Because I'm here. I'm in the room.

Connecting

On Thursday evening, June 22, 2000, three years after I wrote the first draft of this essay, Robert Connors was killed in a motorcycle crash. When I read about it on the WPA listserv, and when I read all of the heartbreaking responses to the news from his colleagues and friends, I felt a curious kind of loss. I'd never met him or studied with him or heard him speak. But some part of me—the lonely part, the one who does not quite want to fit in but still cries when she does not get invited—felt like she knew Robert Connors, or at least one version of him. I'm glad he risked writing something that he must have known would make people like me angry. My anger drove me to seek out others who, in turn, drove me deeper into myself.

Identification, Authority, and Agonistic Discourse

In "The Reproduction of Othering," Laura Brady problematizes early research in feminist composition that relies on the personal narratives of individual women to represent the experiences of all women. Despite feminist scholars' awareness of the problems associated with this kind of essentialist generalizing, Brady explains that the personal narrative continues to function as an appealing rhetorical strategy. Its appeal, she argues, "results from a reading strategy that emphasizes commonality to the exclusion of differences that might problematize the category of woman" (32). In analyses of their respective students' writing, Juanita Rodgers Comfort and Min-Zhan Lu reach a similar conclusion: that female students prefer to read in a way that allows them to identify along gender lines rather than risk disrupting that alliance by attending to differences in race, class, and/or sexual identity. As Lu explains, "their [her students'] interest in confronting sexism is accompanied by a general indifference to the interlocking of sexism with other forms of oppression" ("Reading and Writing," 240).

When I reread Connors's essay now, I see how my revision of it offers further evidence that equating understanding with identification is problematic. That is, in my attempt to understand Connors's argument, I sought to build an alliance in terms that would enable me to identify with it. In order to do so, I *began* with the generalization that an absence of male nurturing causes a certain kind of universal pain. I then used this pain as a way to connect with my male colleagues, and, by extension, Connors himself. However, by striving so hard to identify in this way, I failed to examine other kinds of identifications as well as differences. For example, none of us bothered to wonder if male students *want* to be mentored by their male writing teachers, and, if so, what mentoring might mean to them, and what kinds of wisdom they might find most useful. Additionally, none of my questions asked the participants in my study to reflect on their teacher-student relationships in terms of ethnicity, class, sexual identity, religion, or nationality. In fact, in the search to find some generalizable truths about male teacher-student relationships, I ignored these differences altogether, something which Connors also does and for which he is soundly critiqued (Kirsch, "Comment" 966; Breidenbach, 470–71). Our mutual willingness to ignore these differences is, of course, indicative of our privilege. It is also a testament to my desire to believe in a universal human wound, a pain that transcends all differences. Rather than risk the loss of that belief, I ignored my feminist disciplinary training and, ironically, silenced the very voices that would have made a deep revision of Connors's essay possible. Lacking the knowledges these voices might have helped me make, I rewrote Connors's essay instead of revising it: I added voices that supported his thesis, and I extended his thesis to apply to the women who love these men. "I suffer from the absence of male love, too," the subtext of my version reads, "because when these men are in pain, so am I." Ironically (again), this is the very sort of relational framework contemporary feminist scholars warn me against: When I privilege relationship, I risk giving to others while giving up on myself. "Isn't it time you separated out from a pain that isn't yours?" I hear them asking me. "Isn't it time you did something *else*?"

Could that "something else" be agonistic debate, the very genre Connors heralds, the one I tried so hard to avoid from that start? In yet another ironic turn, Andrea Greenbaum says "yes," arguing that feminist compositionists like me *should* embrace agonistic debate and thereby model for their female students strategies for intervening in public debates on issues that concern them; failure to do so is to remain complicit with the status quo. A curriculum built on care and understanding, Greenbaum continues, will not help women change the structures that oppress them, but a facility for deploying militant arguments can. Greenbaum does note, however, that such a pedagogy is not perfect. That is, while it can help women students develop authority in public discourse, women teachers who practice what she calls "bitch pedagogy" risk negative evaluations from students who expect their female writing teachers to offer a semester of care. In this way, then, the teacher's authority as an effective teacher can be undermined by the very pedagogy that helps her female students assert more authority.

Conversely, according to Connors, the absence of agonistic debate in the classroom has threatened the authority of male teachers, who lack strategies for developing self-confidence in writing programs that advocate more traditionally feminized pedagogies. But the teachers I interviewed contradict this claim, arguing instead that they consciously seek other ways to build teacher authority. Scott, for instance, goes to great lengths to position himself as something other than a man of wisdom, as someone who is learning alongside his students. Ryan "bends like the willow" to give his agonistic male students something less rigid to rebel against. Paul resists reproducing his father's judgmental attitude by "fight[ing] for a more compassionate side." John and Tony connect with the pain expressed by their male students, and employ that connection to help them teach these students about writing. Throughout the interviews, the men I talked with reported a strong disdain for a traditionally masculine style of teaching that foregrounds power differentials between teacher and student. However, like the bitch pedagogists Greenbaum identifies, these men understand the rhetorical effectiveness of confrontation. "Grow up," Scott tells his obnoxiously disruptive student. Furthermore, like women teachers who practice agonistic pedagogies, Scott worries about how his working against an ethic of care will reflect on him as a teacher: Telling that student to grow up is something he would never include in his teaching self-evaluation, he tells us. His resistance to doing so suggests the degree to which both male and female writing teachers working without job security understand the ways power dynamics constrain their ability to practice and teach agonistic discourse.

In different ways, both Connors and Greenbaum lament what is lost when writing teachers feel pressured to abandon the teaching of agonistic discourse. But both authors' arguments also depend on a kind of contextual slippage that deserves further exploration. Connors, for example, in a response to Gesa Kirsch's agonistic critique of his essay, remarks that her "vision of feminism has given her complete permission to throw a pumpkin at my head with all the force she has" ("Comment," 968). Connors contrasts Kirsch's response with one written by a male colleague:

> The differences in tone and presentation between these two responses to my essay are, I think, striking, and they are not unrepresentative of the current state of gendered discourse in the humanities. Patrick McGann, a member of the pro-feminist men's movement, finds elements in my essay he thinks we may disagree about. He is, however, forced by his

rejection of agonistic debate to search—hard and conscientiously—for ways to express himself without falling into traditional male patterns of confrontation. ("Comment," 968)

According to Connors, McGann's resistance to "set [him] straight" is tied to his pro-feminist allegiance. That is, as a man, McGann's performance of agonistic discourse would challenge that allegiance, whereas Kirsch's performance strengthens it. The slippage, however, between this argument and the one Connors advances in his essay concerns context. In his essay, the context is the classroom; in his comment and response, the context is a scholarly publication. In the former, the teacher's primary audience is his students, whereas in the latter the audience is composed of his professional peers. Surely the purposes and effects of agonistic performance must be assessed in light of these changing contexts. Similarly, Greenbaum's contextual slippage between the classroom and public realms outside the classroom suggests the need to rhetorically analyze the purpose of agonistic discourse. Such an analysis can move us beyond some of feminist composition's most resilient binaries—mother/bitch, ethic of care/ agonistic debate—and into a more productive discussion about how we as teachers-scholars might consciously perform these subjectivities and discourses in both our classrooms and our scholarship. (See chapter 5, "Teaching and Learning in Relational Spaces," for further discussion of feminist performance in the classroom.) These two contexts, it seems to me, provide us with a space to self-consciously reflect on our choices of subjectivity and discourse. Doing so is especially crucial in the classroom, where—for reasons that may include but no doubt go beyond gender—diverse students respond differently to different teacher subjectivities, and leading them in an analysis of why this is so seems like something worth doing.

Finally, performing different subjectivities as writing teachers might also help some of us move beyond the rather unproductive goal of proving ourselves to be "good feminists." As someone who identifies as a feminist compositionist, I want to belong, which means I feel pressure to roll my eyes when I hear a conference paper extolling the virtues of an ethic of care. I know that argument is theoretically naïve, even dangerous, but I am not ready to give it up. Such a pedagogy still feels like a form of resistance to me, especially when I teach graduate classes where students have been traumatized by a basic training course in literature (often euphemized as "Introduction to Graduate Study"). For these students, the permission to explore their authentic voices (yes, I just said that), to make connections between what they feel they need to write and what they know they are supposed to write, can feel, well, liberating. I know, because they have told me so. Furthermore, I am unwilling to give up on the need to do emotional work, despite feminist calls to focus elsewhere, because I know there is more emotional work to be done—my own.

My desire to belong as a "good feminist" inevitably influenced my initial reaction to Connors's essay, where the only acceptable response seemed to be a dismissive anger. My attempts to respond differently have been difficult, which suggests the degree to which my identity as a feminist is fixed. However, as Brady and Lu make clear, such rigidity works against the goals of feminism by making reductive identification possible. It also undermines the project of revision, an insight made glaringly apparent by my attempts to revise Connors's essay. Nonetheless, my "failed" multigenre version also created a space that enabled me to hear revision's limits: In contexts of rigid subjectivity, the conditions of allegiance render disruption a threat. As academics, many of us typically deal with these threats by dismissing them through agonistic debate rather than using them as opportunities to examine our investment in the subjectivities they challenge. Consequently, the desire to belong thwarts the project of revision. To be a revisionary rhetor, then, means being willing to risk the pain of repudiation.

Underdeveloped Themes; or, The Diary I Never Wrote

The thing I liked best about my diary was the key. The youngest of five children, I worried about my older brothers, especially M., exposing my secrets, so I hid the key in a place I was sure he would never look: my jewelry box, a plastic, garish thing, home to mood rings and beaded bracelets. (Though now I realize that M. could have pried open the measly lock with a bobby pin and an ounce of effort, and maybe he did.) I began writing in my diary when I was in the second grade and still learning how to steer myself and my hand across the white, untouched page. The cover of the book is itself a marvel: pink and orange large-petaled flowers separated by small white spaces that, somewhere along the line, I saw fit to color in with blue ballpoint pen. In the petals of the center, leftmost flower, I've written my name. Or, what I thought at that time would be my name come eighth-grade confirmation: Julie Marie Elisabeth Jung.

Now I can flip the cover easily to find this penciled scrawl: "What you are about too read I Julie's feelings. I changed the names to protect the inisents. Just Kidding."

As a scholar in rhetoric and composition, I reread this opening disclaimer and am struck by its clear sense of audience: I at eight knowingly address a reader. M.? Myself? Someone with powers to judge and punish? Someone with a sense of humor? Years later, when I would encounter this old diary, usually during moments of transition—while packing boxes to move, let's say—I would reread this inside cover and think that perhaps I envisioned one day reading my diary with my daughter, a fiction yet to materialize, but an audience I nevertheless allow myself to write for even now.

On the second page of my diary, the manufacturer has written in big black letters: "THE PROPERTY OF" and in the line provided my eight-year-old self has written, "me." On the opposite page there is a space to record the year I started writing in my diary: "1974." Below that, where I was supposed to have written the year I stopped writing in it, I've scrawled "I don't care." And on August 4, 1977, at 15 after eight at night, my eleven-year-old self sees fit to revise: "I mean here that 'I don't know.'"

Revisions of this sort are common throughout my diary. I wrote in it on and off for eighteen years, and during many rereadings, my older, embarrassed self could not seem to keep from commenting, re-contextualizing, rationalizing. For example, on July 11, 1977, I write:

Dear Diary it is so queer to write dear diary but I don't know why I do it. I'm bored, man that's the only time I ever write

in here. today I went to the eye doctor I only have to do
my eye exersies three times a week. Yippy. I always talk
about wanting to grow up but when I read this over I don't
want to go on but back up I don't want to change to the
metric system. Bye.

Half of this entry is written in a stilted beginner's cursive, which I
struggle with for eight lines before moving to a more confident print.
Then, in the space reserved for next day's entry, I write the following in a loopy and cocky cursive:

Excuse me. Today is Feb 11, 1979. The Metric System is
easy and fun. So there.

A more striking example of my early revisionist tendencies
begins almost a year later, when I, an eighth grader at St. Charles
Borromeo Catholic Elementary School and a straight A student who
has never kissed a boy, fill two pages as follows:

Awards day tomorrow. Graduation and Kings Island. Beth's
party (kiss Dave?) I love Dave J. I read all those things that
say "I love Larry, Pat" and all these queer things. I'll probably read this in a year and crack up . But, if Dave dumps
me he owes me a dollar. I have to read the petitions at grad
mass. I'm already nervice. I'm going with Dave and I'm
going around with him at Kings Island. I really have to write
down some of my thoughts, so here goes. I love him. I'm
afraid I'll give in to him. But I hope and pray he and I respect each other enough. I pray God will help me stay pure.
I want to be a virgin on my wedding night. So there. But I
love him. He calls me all the time. I wanna kiss him. Bye.

Just under a year later, I did, in fact, reread that entry and crack up,
adding this:

Excuse me, but I must comment on the pure queerness of

that last page. I can't believe I wrote that shit! Well, just thought I'd let you know.

On July 4, 1981, I reconfirm my older, wiser reading and write, "Here, Here!" And just about five years later, as a first-year college student, lonely, homesick, and overwhelmed, I write:

> Today (this weekend) I'm home from school. I'm kind of sick and I have a boatload of homework. (What the hell is going on in Chem? And Calculus max-min problems. God.) After I read this diary I feel like the BIGGEST queer. Well, I'm REALLY IN LOVE NOW. Believe me. It's been D. since January and I love him so much. I go up to Notre Dame to visit him on the 19th. I can't wait. No, I didn't stay pure for my wedding night. Guess I should've given in to Dave J. after all. Jesus Christ, I didn't even kiss the kid!! Gotta go read Henry IV, Part I.

Rereading and structuring this ongoing conversation now, I am moved by the reflective honesty of a young girl who longs to stay young, the awkwardness of a skinny adolescent just on the cusp of her burgeoning sexuality, the lonely musings of a homesick college student. And I'm also struck by the ease with which I discount my own feelings, my own expression, my own experience. "Queer" pops up again and again, a judgment from which no key can protect. The language throughout my diary reveals the nature of my relationship to myself: limited intimacy, temporary honesty. In a way, my diary became a kind of self-contract: I could write about my life only if I agreed that none of it mattered, that none of it was real.

A mentor recently told me that we cannot revise that which is not written. When I reread my diary now, I see the gaps, the erasures, the things I did not say. My very first diary entry, for example, recounts an experience I had at a slumber party the night before:

> March 24, 1974. Today I came home from Kelly's and just becous we where talking a little Kelly had to get wipped.

and Troy got 8 pancakes and we only got 2 and Kelly saind can I have some more pancakes and her mom saind no I'll tell you what you can have more of and you already got it once *and I am terrified that a parent can beat a child at her own birthday party and I remember the day Kelly came to school with two broken arms and then I hear the crack of the belt and Kelly's screams and later she comes back to the room and everyone is quiet until I hear her cry and I don't know what to say, except I want to cry, too, and I want to go home so bad and at breakfast I can't eat and then mom picks me up and I run to the car and lock the door and she asks, "how was it?" and I say, "fine," and at home I go straight to my room and unlock my diary and try to write everything down but it won't come out right because my handwriting is too wide and I think I'm only allowed to fill one page, but I don't worry so much because I think, "if I write this down—this much, at least— I'll remember it always."*

Entries like these occur sporadically throughout my diary. They say just enough to make me remember specific moments from my childhood, and when I reread them, these moments become so vivid and clear that my current memory merges with actual event; the two transcend time and space and fuse into one; through language past is made now and my life is made whole.

In a later entry I gloss over the first time (one of only two times) I saw my mom cry.

And then there are the times about which I write nothing at all. But even for these my diary focuses me, reminds me of a season or an attitude, and asks me to remember what I can:

February 14, 1976. Happy Valentines Day. I'm all better. I still got the sniffles. Sniff sniff! I want to be a pro basket-ball player when I'm bigger. I played with M. and S. with basket ball but they always fight. I also play with Jill. We got a hamster named Dudley. It's a girl. (We got her about a week ago). Bye! *And during days like these, these glimpses of the spring yet to come, when S. and M. are so happy to be outside that they even let me play with them, it's during one of these kinds of days that M. tries to hang himself in the tree in the front yard and I cut him down with the hedge clippers (did I?) and I can't remember feeling anything and I don't remember Mom and Dad doing anything. And now when I ask L. about it she says she doesn't remember it even happening and S. says he remembers but that it was no big deal because M. just wanted some attention and M., he lives alone and is miserable still and he calls me out of the blue last week (he never calls anyone) and says he's having trouble sleeping and I tell him to drink chamomile tea but I don't say "I love you" and I never do.*

Maybe these moments, and there were others like them, never made it into my diary because I didn't have the language to express them. But I doubt that. I think what I didn't have was the means to revise them. In the face of such pain and despair, my reader, and her "this is so queer" commentary, found herself out of her league. Moments like these violated that unspoken self-contract: They made my life matter; they made it too real for words.

If it is true that we can revise only what is written, maybe it is also true that we can write only what has been revised. I think of my first-year college students who come to me during my office hours. They tell me they're confused about the essay assignment and, to convince me, they reach into gargantuan backpacks and pull out binders over-flowing with handouts and syllabi. I watch, amused. I enjoy young writers *so much.* And when we finally get to talking, they tell me about their families, their friends. They say how different college is from high school, and they confess that they worry about flunking out. Last summer, one student described in vivid detail a party he attended the weekend before, a party where a friend of his was shot. "You ever seen how somebody's hand shakes when he's holdin' a gun, Miss?"

he asks. "No," I answer. I think of my childhood, growing up in the idyllic peace of suburban Ohio. "No. I've never even seen a gun before." He looks incredulous, but he goes on.

They tell me all this and more, but they don't write it. And although I ask them to explore issues that matter to them, those that feel important in their own lives, most of them do not. Most of them remain disengaged and unchanged. They pick topics they've already researched and they write neat and tidy conclusions that paint a cheery picture of the world. When I ask them to revise "to find a more meaningful purpose" (a phrase I write a lot at the end of student papers), they typically fix their typos. I used to think these students were lazy or too busy rushing and going to parties to take their writing seriously. But now I am in the process of rethinking my students' silences. Through the lens of my diary, they take on new meaning, one that forces me to confront my own. And I hear all of these silences speaking to me now, asking me again and again: Why make real by putting into words those experiences we feel we are powerless to change?

My answer is that by writing our silences, we do, in fact, change them. We change them because we change ourselves. And in the process we are granted a most unexpected gift: a reader who is unafraid.

5 / Teaching and Learning in Relational Spaces

A Teacher's Story

Last semester I taught a graduate level seminar I had recently designed called "Rhetorics of Scholarship—Writing for Publication," with the intent both to help students prepare manuscripts for submission and to make (dis)connections across the subfields in English studies of interest to the graduate students who enrolled. Nine of the enrolled students were women; one was male. Of the nine women, four had completed my seminar in "Feminist Composition" the semester before and were eager to continue revising for publication drafts begun in that course. I was looking forward to the chance to continue working with these students, as our "Feminist Composition" class was the sort of community that forms only rarely—we shared many "A-HA" moments, lots of laughter, and a great deal of provocative, challenging writing. Continuing that community, if only in part, was something I very much desired, but I also realized that its remaining unchanged—with a new course design and five new students, to say the least—would be impossible. On the first day, I walked in a little late, admitting to having gotten lost in the halls and going to the wrong classroom. This subjectivity, which I call The Fool, is one I perform often in my undergraduate and graduate classes, sometimes despite my better judgment. Although I like to start classes off with laughter, especially on the first day when anxiety typically runs high, I also realize from experience that students who might challenge my position of authority—that is, my bodily presence as a youngish, female authority—are the ones least likely to be charmed by this performance. On this particular day, I remember my former students laughing, as they were

...iliar with my Fool, but I also noticed that the one male student did not look in my direction; instead, he read something at his desk, which I shortly thereafter realized was the schedule of English graduate classes offered that semester. I decided for the time being to ignore what he was doing, telling myself that different students use different strategies to get through anxious classroom moments and using a text to "check out" seemed like something a person in English might do.

I began as I always do: I asked the students to write. For this particular course, I asked them to write about the subjects of their proposed manuscripts as well as any genre and audience concerns. I explained that after writing we would use our texts as springboards to introduce ourselves and our projects for the term. As I settled down to write along with them, I noticed that that same student, whom I will call Devon, was still reading his schedule of classes and was not making a move to begin writing. My immediate responses to his behavior were mixed. On the one hand, I told myself, he can do—or not do—whatever he wants. He's a graduate student, an adult, for godssakes, and I wasn't about to "make" him write if he didn't want to. Beneath this laissez faire cover, however, I was seething. I despise being put in the position of having to discipline students, especially graduate students. I also felt insulted, wondering as I tried to write about my own project if this student would dare do such a thing in the classrooms of more senior male faculty. His chosen text also clearly communicated to me that he did not take my course seriously, a sentiment driven home by his decision to ignore my request. Ultimately what I think I felt most was a sense of responsibility to my other students. I felt strongly that if we were going to develop a writing community, then everyone needed to write; opting out from doing so on day one was bound to generate resentment from those who took the task seriously, and I decided then that I would confront Devon publicly so as to communicate to the group that *not* writing was not an option.

What I did next I have never seen a teacher do in a classroom. The only model I had to work from was my former therapist, who confronted me on more than one occasion with a compassionate strength I have not experienced often since. In that moment, I did my best to summon her spirit, performing a therapist subjectivity that was neither Rogerian nor Noddingesque. Instead, I announced that I very much wanted to hear about people's projects, but first I needed to clear the air.

"Devon," I said, "I noticed you didn't write anything and instead have been reading a list of courses, which makes me question your commitment to this particular course."

In response, he started gathering his things and said something like, "I guess I better leave then."

Surprised and disappointed, as I had hoped my comments would generate a productive conversation, not shame him into immediate departure, I explained that I wasn't asking him to leave the class, only to explore if he intended to remain in it. At this point, he asked if he could talk with me privately. I hesitated. I had only just met some of the other students in the class; conferencing one-on-one with him seemed like special treatment. Still, my gut instinct told me his concerns needed to be addressed immediately, so I agreed. I asked my four former students, whose projects I was already familiar with, to begin the discussion while Devon and I stepped out.

In an empty classroom next door, Devon explained that he was questioning whether the class was right for him based on past experiences in other graduate seminars. We spent about thirty minutes discussing his concerns, all of which sounded legitimate to me. It was also clear that Devon had done quite a bit of hard thinking about his decision and that his behavior in class was not meant to be insulting but was rather the consequence of some troubling circumstances. The specific narrative of these circumstances is Devon's story to tell. Suffice it to say that what troubled me most was Devon's fear that his arguments, some of which challenged feminist commonplaces, would not be well heard in my classroom. Given my almost obsessive commitment to listening well, I tried to persuade Devon that I would make every effort to create a classroom space where competing perspectives could be voiced. I also emphasized my belief in the need for productive discomfort to facilitate revision. Although his remaining in the course would no doubt generate some tension, I told him that I believed its presence would benefit us all. By destroying the comfort zones that mark ideological rigidity, his competing perspective would force us all to think more deeply.

Devon mulled over my points with a sincerity I considered genuine. He then asked if he could wait a week to decide. I agreed, but I also said that should he choose to remain in the course, he would need to share with the whole class the concerns he had expressed to me privately. This request floored him. "That's not something I could ever do," he said. Although I said I understood his hesitation, I also explained that unless his concerns were made public—unless they became a text we as a community could construct, revise, and integrate—they would assume control of the course like so many pink elephants.

"Everyone in that room knows we've been in here talking for a half-hour," I said. "If you stay in the class, our conversation will affect them, which means they have a right to know about it."

We then rejoined the others. Later that week Devon called to let me know he had decided to drop the course in favor of pursuing his project as an independent study with another professor. I thanked him for the update, reaffirmed my interest in his research topic, and, because I was already feeling utterly exhausted that term, breathed a huge sigh of relief.

From my perspective, Devon's departure from the course generated a kind of women-only solidarity that both advanced and undercut my course goals. On the one hand, the space we created over the next few weeks was of the sort that I have experienced only among women. We laughed a lot. We supported each other's writing with nurturing encouragement and intellectual finesse. Those in the class writing creative nonfiction pieces plunged bravely into the painful specifics of eating disorders, body image, cultural and sexual identity, family, love. Others writing more traditional scholarly pieces used contemporary feminist rhetorical and literary theories to examine specific classroom experiences where their presence as women intellectuals was both ignored and ridiculed. I doubt very much that these students could have mined their memories so deftly if Devon had remained in the course, but maybe I'm wrong.

On the other hand, as the weeks passed I felt a kind of fatigue that is particular to boredom. I was tired of agreeing, tired of getting along. Mostly, though, I was tired of being so nice. My former therapist used to talk about this in our weekly women's group—how we were all so very nice, none of us willing to get angry or even disagree.

"That's the biggest challenge with women's groups," she used to say, "getting them to stop being so damn nice all the time."

To be sure, had Devon remained in the course, there would have been ample opportunity to get mean. But, as the only man in a strongly feminist group, he may have become an easy scapegoat. Instead, in his absence, the other women in the class and I had only each other should face-to-face confrontation become necessary. And thankfully, ultimately, it did.

Near the middle of the term, I started complaining to a friend about the class's tendency to "blow off" assignments I thought I had been quite clear in requiring. For example, because the course functioned mostly as a writing workshop, I stressed the importance of committing to manuscript due dates. Together we agreed that students being workshopped would email their drafts no later than Wednesday, thereby giving the rest of us ample time to read, digest, and write review letters for class the following Monday night. To help us comment meaningfully, I also required students to attach analyses of their target journals and cover sheets describing their writing processes and listing specific questions regarding their drafts.

Although several of the students dutifully met all these requirements on a regular basis, others did not. Drafts were emailed late, causing me to have to revise my own research schedule in order to find time to respond. (Although I flirted with the idea of offering no response, I couldn't muster the nerve. For possible explanations as to why, see The Martyr and The New Professor, below.) Some drafts showed up without cover sheets or journal analyses. Annoyed, I begrudgingly sent out reminder emails and then hoped I had time to read and respond before class. In general, I am strongly opposed to the concept of giving people—particularly professional colleagues—"reminders"; we're all busy; we all struggle to balance competing responsibilities. Some of us keep day runners or palm pilots; others develop wonderful memories. I have no patience for those who believe they are entitled to be reminded of obligations the rest of us labor to keep track of ourselves. (The expectation that one is due a reminder is, in my experience, classed and gendered. I once worked for a composition director who asked me repeatedly to remind him of upcoming meetings. "Why?" I would ask. "Just write a note in your day planner. That's what I do.") As a teacher, I hand out reminders more freely, given that many of my undergraduate students are just learning to keep track of their newly hectic schedules. However, I expect more from graduate students, not the least of which is the knowledge that a course syllabus is all the text a competent graduate student needs to remind herself of what is due and when.

Because all of the students in this particular seminar far exceeded basic competency, I struggled to understand their failure to meet with the listed requirements. Interestingly, my initial and strongest response was very similar to the way I reacted to Devon's refusal to write during our first class meeting—I felt personally insulted.

"These students think I'm a pushover," I complained to my friend. "They think I'm cool, that I won't care if they blow things off."

As I said this, I was reminded of an episode during my own graduate schooling, when a teacher whom I very much admire told me how angry she was that students in our seminar presented their final papers as if they were "works in progress."

"Did I ever say that your final papers could be rough drafts?" she asked.

"No, " I answered honestly. "You were very clear that they should be final versions."

Remembering that incident, I connected our experiences as graduate writing teachers who value revision and are attentive to process. My interpretive context shifted then from the personal to the institutional, and I became angry for feminist writing teachers everywhere. As I did with Devon, I told myself these students would not dare treat more senior male professors with such disrespect.

Furthermore, I was furious that teachers like me and my mentor—
who work so hard to communicate our respect for our students—
are often treated so disrespectfully in return.

"Why bother?" I asked myself. "Why bother doing all this extra work trying to practice feminist pedagogy when being an asshole
is so much easier—and is respected more?"

This last point was particularly painful, given that the class was
composed of all women, most of whom publicly identified as feminists. I felt betrayed by a community I had expected to sustain me.
If feminist graduate students could not be made to value the kind
of class I was trying to create, then who would?

"These students are persuading me to practice patriarchy," I
finally told my friend. "And they need to know that."

At this point, I would like to interrupt my narrative to call attention to a few of the competing, intersecting, and overlapping identities I observe circulating within it. Taken together, they represent how I see myself and many others I know moving through the
world as women/feminists/RhetComp people. While their sheer
plurality disrupts the mother/bitch, nurturing care/agonistic debate binaries that construct and limit me as a feminist teacher-
scholar, they, too, feel fixed to me, emerging as rigid subidentities
rather than as revisable subjectivities. In an effort to dislodge their
sense of permanency, I give them names and describe qualities I
associate with each. By examining these parts of my experience as
I would characters in a play, I hope to move beyond the rigid boundaries of identity and into experiencing subjectivity as rhetorical
performance.

The Hard Ass
Enjoys confronting shady mechanics and public transit gropers. Has
zero tolerance for those whose actions mark them as privileged.
Fears being taken advantage of by students and colleagues alike. Is
not afraid of people saying things like, "Jeez, what a hard ass." In
fact, kind of likes it.

The Injured Party
Is never treated the way she deserves. Always gives more than she
gets. Frequently feels insulted or let down. Has been abused in the
past, usually by men. Is full of rage. Yells at slow drivers, unfocused
check-out cashiers, and pesky toddlers. Thinks there's nothing
wrong with really, *really* high expectations. Complains about atro-
cious student writing with friends who sympathize.

The Martyr
Heavy sigh. Has stacks and stacks of papers to read, too much committee work, and several research projects of her own that she can't
get to because, sigh, her students need their papers back. Is a de-
voted gym rat but workload demands that she abandon exercise for
the months of October–mid-December and February–mid-May.
During these months she eats take-out and drinks too much beer.
This helps explain why she gains weight, her face breaks out, and
she starts to forget things. Unself-consciously and liberally uses the
phrasing "makes me," as in: "My students are making me postpone
my own research," and "You're making me feel fat." Dismisses concerns voiced by friends with a flip of the wrist and a smug sense of
self-importance. Wrongly believes in her own indispensability.

The Process Goddess
Believes in the power of dialogue. Loves reading rough drafts, hates
grading final versions. Is addicted to students' potential. Says things
like "We're all on a journey" and "It's okay to get angry in class."
Fearlessly assigns personal narratives. Feels her special gift is connecting with the wounded spirits of damaged students. Thinks
people who bash Expressivism really just need a good therapist.
Fantasizes about shaving head and becoming a Buddhist monk.

The Equalizer
Never introduces herself as "Dr." Has no signature line listing title
and credentials on email account. Secretly mocks people who do.
(Does, however, have diploma framed and hanging in office.) Re-

fuses offers to relocate to a bigger office. Writes along with students. Brings own writing in to share with students. Says anyone can get a Ph.D. as long as s/he's willing to go $50,000 in debt. Makes a point to befriend secretaries and janitors. Is afraid of her own privilege.

The Envyist

Thinks literature professors—especially senior white male professors—have the world's easiest job. Fantasizes about delivering brilliant lectures in some knowable content area. Yearns to walk into a room and command respect without having to prove anything first. Believes students in these classes take copious notes and hand papers in on time. Imagines assigning novels and sitting around talking about them as sheer luxury. Wonders what it must be like to feel no compunction to stay current or to do work that improves the world. Resents these professors' refusal to shoulder some of the department's emotional weight (as in, "I bet nobody ever shows up crying to *their* office!"). Has never actually talked with these professors about their teaching, nor has she ever sat in on any of their classes, but is sure she is right.

The Dummy

Feels inadequate among department's literary "theory heads." Is embarrassed to admit she has never read *Moby Dick, Ulysses,* or anything by Virginia Woolf other than parts of *A Room of One's Own.* Reads canonical classics during the summer but worries she's not "getting it." Winces when new graduate students say things like, "Oh, so you do pedagogy, right?" Wishes regularly that she were more articulate. Worries that her frequent boisterous laughter makes her appear giggly and stupid. Vows to be more serious.

The New Prof/Orphaned Grad Student

Is trying hard to prove she deserved to be hired. Worries frequently that she'll be fired. Is way behind in reading back issues of *College English* and *CCC.* Feels like a fraud. Wonders what exactly her "specialty" is, anyway. Misses the praise and A's received in grad school.

Rereads old seminar papers and thinks, "God, I was so smart then." Frequently contemplates going to medical and/or law school. Over-extends credit—again—buying overpriced but seemingly appropriately professorial clothes from J. Crew. Looks at butt in mirror before going to teach class.

When the day arrived to confront my class, I was ready. Because I had not received the draft of one student due to be workshopped (see Zoé's reflection below), I was feeling especially angry, and I also knew we would have extra time. At the start of the second half of the seminar, after a short break, I began by asking the students to brainstorm qualities they associated with classes that do not practice feminist pedagogy. For lack of a better term, I wrote on the chalkboard, "Patriarchal Pedagogy." Together we generated a list that looked something like this:

Patriarchal Pedagogy
Teacher is expert; students are novices; reinforces teacher/ student binary;

Teacherly presence is dominating, authoritarian, fear-inducing;

Teacher lectures and uses banking method, shame-based pedagogies;

Assignments and classroom experiences are acontextual, aprocess;

Classroom does not feel like a safe place.

One student remarked that sometimes in such courses lip service is paid to respecting students' ideas and opinions but that in reality these classes are what she termed "fake spaces": Everyone in them knows the truth, which is that the teacher is right, is in control.

We then created a list to describe qualities that characterize a class founded on feminist pedagogy. Not surprisingly, given the way I initiated the discussion, most of the qualities generated were the binary opposites of those appearing in our first list:

Feminist Pedagogy

Is egalitarian, community-based;

Values what each person "brings to the table" in terms of experience, expertise;

Is attentive to process, context;

Adopts discussion or workshop format;

Respects situated knowledges;

Co-constructs knowledge among teacher and students; disrupts teacher/student binary.

After generating these lists, I explained that I felt very strongly about valuing the unique experiences and knowledges each student in the class brought to our table, and I circled the room, identifying each of these. I then took a deep breath and said, "What I'm about to say is hard, but despite my efforts to value your expertise, I don't feel as if you are honoring mine in return."

At this most of the students looked genuinely baffled, so I pressed on, explaining that I had developed the syllabus and its requirements based on my expertise in teaching and studying rhetoric and writing and that in failing to comply with these assignments my students were, in fact, telling me my expertise "wasn't worth shit." I also told them that their behavior was "persuading me to abandon feminist pedagogy and practice patriarchy," given that the former did not seem to work, even among committed feminists.

I remember a brief silence, and then one student started to explain why she had not done some of the assignments. Her reasons made sense. For example, her journal analysis had not been completed because she had not yet picked her target journal. Another student explained that she had been having computer problems and that was why her draft was emailed late. I listened to these explanations and others like them and slowly realized that, shockingly, none of them had anything to do with me. Incredulous that this could actually be the case, I asked, "Come on. Don't you kind of blow things off in my class because you think I'm cool? Do you do these sorts of things in senior male professors' classes?"

A few students nodded yes, they did (although another said, "Well, the squeaky wheel gets the grease," meaning, I suppose, that the consistently hard-assed types are "obeyed" more readily than wafflers like me).

Although I was persuaded that the students' reasons were in fact reasonable, I nevertheless argued that they had a responsibility to the class community to explain why they were missing deadlines and ignoring requirements. Because feminist pedagogy is attentive to process, teachers and students alike need to be able to revise deadlines and expectations as circumstances change, but these revisions must be processed with the group and not decided on an individual basis.

"Otherwise," I said, "some of us go off feeling insulted and resentful."

At this point, a few of the students who dutifully met the required deadlines spoke for the first time, describing their feelings of resentment toward those who felt entitled to ignore the needs and expectations of the community. One of the students said *she* felt personally responsible when another's draft did not get emailed to her on time; she worried that perhaps she had accidentally deleted it or that her computer was on the fritz. Another student remarked that she "felt horrible, just horrible" when she did not have enough time to review a late draft thoroughly before class. These students' comments helped me realize that I was not alone in personalizing my reactions to late or missing emails. Furthermore, they dramatized for me how a teacher-initiated confrontation can help students voice their own frustrations and resentments as well.

I remember then that one student, who had for some time seemed physically uncomfortable in her seat, spoke up, saying something like, "Well, I know this might not go over well, but I feel like what you just did was create a fake space."

Basically, as I remember it, her point was that while I had seemingly initiated a "discussion" of feminist vs. patriarchal teaching methods, what I had really done was lectured to and shamed them, ironically employing the very teaching strategies I rail against.

Her comment stopped me cold. Had I really done that? I knew this student was angry, something I had expected, given that confrontation is never a pleasurable experience for those being confronted. And now there I sat, suddenly in the position of confrontee myself.

I considered her comment carefully and then said that I believed my opening was genuine—I really did want to hear what they had to say about the different kinds of pedagogies. I also said that my hurt feelings, borne from what felt like their disrespect, were not fake but were in fact quite real and painful to me.

Another student, Marie, who had been researching shame pedagogy all term, chimed in that sometimes shame is an appropriate feeling to have—as in cases where we have done something for which we *should* feel ashamed.

Zoé then turned to me and gently asked, "Why didn't you start that way, then, with your feelings, instead of with the different pedagogies? Didn't you think your feelings were good enough?"

Again, I was stopped cold. As someone who professes the value of mining feelings to yield potentially transformative knowledge, I could not believe I had unknowingly buried my own beneath some dispassionate brainstorming exercise.

I expressed all this aloud, trying to understand in front of them why I had begun as I did, and I concluded that maybe I had done so because I wanted them to see my situation within a larger context of being a feminist teacher in an institution where, despite considerable changes, traditional pedagogies still dominate. I explained that none of my feminist teachers had ever made their own struggles part of the classroom experience, and by doing so myself I was hoping to help them when their turn came. I wanted them to know that their future resentments and frustrations as feminist teachers were not unique to them but were shared by many of us and that maybe by talking about our problems with each other we could find the energy to continue.

As class came to an end, I felt extremely disconnected from the student who had confronted me most directly—the one who had accused me of creating a fake space. I felt an enormous urge to smooth things over with her, to "make nice," but I also knew that doing so would keep us from hearing each other fully, so I resisted. I silently told myself that it was okay if she left class angry, and if I did, too. In that moment, I realized something that felt to me deeply profound, and I said it aloud to the class: By confronting me, this student had helped me realize that my feminist pedagogy *was* working, that our space was, in fact, not fake; otherwise, she never would have said aloud in class—to me directly—what she did. I thanked her for her courage and for risking our connection, and, because time was running out, I asked the students to continue thinking about all we had said and to write about it, talk about it, in future classes.

Although the subject never came up again during class, students did begin to email each other and me with explanations for delayed manuscripts. Other students began asking for acknowledgments that their emailed drafts had gotten through. Several of the students wrote about that class period in their end-of-semester reflective letters, telling me that it was a powerful experience, one they appreciated more as the semester continued. Still, I was somewhat disappointed that as a whole we never discussed that day together. I worried that our collective silence meant that something had gone wrong. And then I regrouped, reminding myself that sometimes silence is what we need.

Three Students' Stories

The following reflections of the classroom experiences I narrate above are written by three graduate students who enrolled in both my Feminist Composition seminar (where we read and discussed Andrea Greenbaum's "Bitch Pedagogy"; for a discussion of this article, see chapter 4) and the "Rhetorics of Scholarship" course; they were also in class on the days when these experiences took place. In an email inviting these students to share their own stories, I wrote the following:

> Would you be willing to write something on how you experienced those particular class periods, and/or how your learning about feminist pedagogy has affected you as a thinker, writer, student, teacher, woman, person, etc.? For example, how do you (or do you) think your identity/subjectivity as

a STUDENT is affected when a teacher deploys different kinds of feminist pedagogy? I'm thinking we in my field always talk of "the student" as something solid and coherent, but we all know that's not true. What are some of the student identities that can be "born" when a teacher allows her teacher identity to be fluid and in-process? And why am I reaffirming this student/teacher binary? What complexities result when THAT boundary breaks down, and what can we learn from the resulting pain, confusion? Those are just some questions to get you thinking. Others are most welcome, especially the ones I haven't thought to ask.

Marie Moeller, "Epiphany of a Cynic: Feminist Pedagogy and Its Fluidity"

I spent a long time in classrooms learning what I did not want to do as a teacher. Most people remember the teachers who made a difference in their lives, and I do remember those, but the moments that vividly stick in my head are the ones where I can remember saying, "I don't think I'll ever do that as a teacher." Then I went to graduate school, became a teacher (in the very formal sense of the word), and found out how easy it is to become complacent, taking the easy road, doing what is expected of me. I was expected, by my students, even by my co-teachers, to be a mother, to be the sort of teacher who is caring, nurturing, and never raises her voice to anyone. But, from that stereotype, I also found that my students expected me to spoon-feed them information, to practically (if not totally) do their work for them, and give them A's without a second thought, just because they are nice people. That's not what I wanted. I *do* care. I *am* warm, which I guess makes me the prototype for that sort of stereotype, but I did not set out to create a world full of overly dependent people. I performed my role, quite well in fact, until my second year of graduate school, when I encountered an article, and a professor, who introduced me to feminist pedagogy. It's not perfect, it has its faults just like anything else, but for me, the benefits, both for myself as a teacher, as a student, and for my students themselves, definitely outweigh the difficulties that come with feminist pedagogy.

During our first session of "Rhetorics of Scholarship," which I took the last semester of my master's program, we were asked to freewrite about the project we wished to work on in class. There was one student, however, who I had noticed at the beginning of class wasn't quite paying attention to anything the professor or students were saying. Instead, he was perusing the course catalog, giving us the impression that he really was not interested in his project, or in any of ours, which in a workshop setting can be devastating to all participants. As a student, I felt a twinge of disgust set in as I thought, "I hope he finds another class in that stupid course catalog he insists on leafing through." As a teacher I thought, "What a nightmare. What would I do with this student?" I'd encountered students like this before and have had them ruin my classes. I had never known what to do with them. Nothing I tried worked. I watched my professor with intent eyes, very curious to see what tool I could learn from her. I had taken a course with her the semester before, had learned her mannerisms, and the way that she dealt with different situations. Each course, I realized, each semester, each day, is different, and in this course, on the first day, I recognized my professor using different instructional techniques than in my previous course with her.

Before we started to discuss our project writings, my professor turned to this individual and said,

> To start, I think I'd like _____ to go first. I couldn't help but notice that during our freewriting exercise, you were looking at the course catalog and not participating in our activity, which says to me that you really aren't interested or invested in this course, which if that is the case, I might suggest that this may not be the course for you.

My jaw, as a student, dropped to the ground. As a teacher, the little voice inside of me yelled, "Yes, yes, yes!" and began to jump up and down in a dance of celebration. As I watched that student clamor for a response (which he obviously did not anticipate from this particular professor), my fellow classmates and I looked at each other in disbelief and admiration for this professor who had finally done what I, as a feminist and a teacher, had wanted to do many times throughout my years as a teacher. She had been assertive, but, more important, she had responded to a situation in the way that she felt appropriate and most beneficial instead of succumbing to roles which perhaps were presumed by this student who knew the name of feminist pedagogy, knew that the professor believed in such a pedagogy, but made his own assumptions about the foundations of such a pedagogy.

As my professor and this individual stepped out into the hall, I began to think about feminist pedagogy and how in one instance I learned it is all right to be fluid in both your identity as a teacher and your actions as an instructor. I also finally came to understand what feminist pedagogy meant to me in that moment. I could be assertive and nurturing, and everything in-between, but each situation is different, and to accurately learn and use feminist pedagogy, one must read each situation and respond accordingly. My professor's example allowed me to become more aware, both of the actions and their interpretations in my classrooms and of my reactions and interpretations in my own classrooms. I became a believer that day and have noticed fewer moments in my classrooms (and in others) when I say to myself, "I'd never do that . . ."

Teryn J. Robinson, "Bitch: Understanding Feminist Pedagogy"

In some students' minds, the label "bitch" is right on target when we're talking about a teacher employing bitch pedagogy. I've seen students, the kinds of students who get defensive when they're called on what they've been doing wrong, mutter "what a bitch" under their breaths. I've seen students turn defensive quickly when they thought a teacher's lecture targeted them or when it did single them out. I've seen them shocked, not believing the teacher capable of such an action, not believing a teacher would single out a student for wasting everyone's time.

I think that if I hadn't read Andrea Greenbaum's essay "Bitch Pedagogy," I would have been one of those students in the parking lot after class saying, "I can't believe she [our teacher] was such a bitch tonight." I would have been one of those shocked students when my kind, supportive teacher turned, well, assertive.

"Assertive" is the first word I think of when anyone mentions bitch pedagogy. I think of a teacher doing what she has to do for herself and for the benefit of the course and students. I think of a teacher who isn't out there to embarrass anyone or make anyone angry. Instead, I think of a teacher who sees something going off track, a teacher who is thinking about what she can do to fix things in a way that can benefit as many people as possible.

On the first night of our "Rhetorics of Scholarship" class, Julie stopped a problem in its early stages. By asking a student—who was leafing through the course listings for the semester instead of writing—why he wasn't participating, she sent the message to him—and to the rest of the class—that this wasn't going to be the kind of class where you could be disinterested; a workshop is the kind of course where everyone really needs to be involved. Weeks later, when Julie led us in a discussion of the struggles of a feminist teacher—struggles she was enduring—she didn't intend just to make those who were slacking in their participation and commitment to our workshop feel bad. She began a discussion that was to be more productive than name-calling and finger-pointing. Sure, the problems with the course came up, but the bigger issues of her struggles were the important part of the discussion. Instead of just sitting back and letting problems persist and irritate her, Julie started conversations—with one student and with the whole class—that took a lot of courage. She confronted a problem, not the students, and asked us what we could do, what we could all do, to work on the problem, because it wasn't a problem that belonged to any one person.

Bitch pedagogy is not about being aggressive toward students. It's about being assertive in confronting trouble spots in the classroom and finding ways to solve problems. I think studying bitch pedagogy made Julie a better problem solver and a better facilitator. I think it did the same for those of us who knew what was going on when Julie employed the method of teaching to its highest degree. We didn't just jump to our name-calling ("bitch") out of ignorance or defensiveness. Instead, I think I've become a better teacher. I'm not afraid to say to my students, "I think this isn't working, so I want your input on what we can do to make things work better." When I was working on my teaching degree as an undergraduate, I was taught students will pounce on weakness, but I'm not afraid of my students anymore. And, I'm learning to not be afraid of the problems we encounter. As a mentor, Julie has taught me it's okay to be frustrated and to turn that frustrated energy into something constructive by being assertive and honest with my students.

Zoé Younker, "'What ya' talkin' about, bitch!?' A Real Student in a Real Class that got Real Confrontational"

Graduate school was the first time I took a feminist class. I walked in with the basic preconceived notions of what a feminist class would be. Probably all lesbians with bad haircuts and furry legs. I guess I was a feminist in the sense that I had had the courage and ambition to be the first woman from my family to graduate from a university. I had a career in public relations and I hated ironing shirts. But I also would never have called myself a "feminist" in public. I like to wear dresses and shave my legs. I'm married. I can't possibly be a feminist.

But I jumped into the [Feminist Composition] course full force. Some of the issues we discussed in class where easier to understand than the others. And some of the research I did for a group project allowed me to research more Latina feminist rhetoric, which I think helped center my own identity. One of the readings that was somewhat of a highlight was "Bitch Pedagogy." The term itself was such a riot, so liberating but at the same time so naughty. It made me feel like I was in the third grade again. Bitch Pedagogy. BITCH Pedagogy. BITCH!

After I finished reading it, I felt somewhat ashamed. I had stopped talking to my high school mentor after I had visited her house on a Sunday and she had asked her husband to tell me she

wasn't home. I also felt bad for calling other female teachers
"bitches" when they had not fulfilled the role of a nurturing mother;
most of all I wondered if Julie was trying to send a message since I
felt I had also started to gravitate to her as a nurturer. I was sure that
she was asking us to "back off" emotionally.

In class we discussed the dichotomy that teachers face as either
bitches or mothers. We also focused on political issues that women
face in the academy, such as still being paid seventy-nine cents to a
man's dollar and, more important, sometimes failing to get tenure.
A classmate mentioned that, for a woman, teaching is a lot like social service—you have to make sure you don't get drained and still
take care of yourself. After a long discussion of the need to find the
balance between being a teacher, nurturer, mother, friend, colleague,
bitch, and all the other titles we carry into the classroom, Julie invited us out for a beer.

Sitting at Lunker's, a pub near the school, we discussed more
sensitive subjects, such as our partners, sexuality, and the times
classmates had "come out" of the closet. I couldn't help but bask in
the irony. Here Julie was throwing everything we had discussed in
class out the window. That night I posted this message on our course
webboard:

Topic: A PROBLEMATIC CLASS (1 of 3), Read 20 times
Conf: FEMINIST COMPOSITION
From: ZOE YOUNKER
Date: Friday, November 02, 2001
Throughout the class, we have had conversations about how
students (and colleagues) perceive the role of a feminist. I think
Julie does a great job at problematizing the word, especially
when she dresses "hip." Is it possible to be fashionable and be a
feminist?

Also, last night we discussed the need to set boundaries with
students and to understand you can't always be a mother or be a
friend . . . then we go out for drinks.

The fact that I am constantly reflecting on society and my
personal ideals is a very refreshing aspect of the course. But it

makes me wonder if this course would be as successful if we had a professor with a different personality or teaching style.

I got the following response from Teryn:

I've been thinking about Zoé's post for a few days now, and I've been trying to figure out what I want to post as my reply (because I really felt like I wanted to reply) . . . I don't think I've quite figured out what I want to say, so let's consider my post as a work in progress.

Thinking about clothes leads me to thinking about beauty. My life hasn't been the same since I read Naomi Wolf's *The Beauty Myth.* I was never someone who really cared all that much for makeup, but reading Wolf's book really showed me (perhaps put into specific words general thoughts of mine) how ideas of what is beautiful work against women. The professor who assigned the text to me taught me a lot that semester (a few years ago) about beauty and feminism and how they interact. She taught me a valuable point: your actions really do affect others (something folks like Britney Spears have yet to learn, in my opinion). I learned that the things I do to my body come from the influences of the world around us and affect the same people in that world. My professor taught me to be conscious of the things I do. I stopped shaving my legs after taking her class. It was a hard decision to make (then, in the days when I starved myself to wear short skirts) because of the implications it has for beauty. Could I be beautiful if I didn't shave my legs? Lots of pressure came in from all around me telling me I couldn't be beautiful that way, and for awhile I gave in and did shave them. For me, though, it's an issue of bravery—can I be brave enough not to do it so that other women can see that they don't have to buy into that idea of beauty? After a few years, the answer became "Yes, yes I can do this for the good of other women."

In a culture like ours that is so wrapped up in what it means to be beautiful, I think it can be really difficult to be a feminist teacher. Each time this fall when I wore shorts to class, I wondered what my students were thinking. Each day, I was aware of my body. I was defying their ideas of what a woman should be, and how would that affect us? Did it make me a "radical" or "angry"? Did it make me a dyke? Did it affect the respect they had/have for me? I was always self-conscious, but I wore my shorts anyway because I was making a statement. If even one of my 11 female students questioned for one day whether or not she needed to subscribe to the traditional notions of beauty, then I'm glad I did what I did.

And, I'm not afraid to wear a dress, either, because I do think I have the right to (just like I have the right to walk home alone at night or to wear what I want to a party or to say "no"). Wearing a dress for me has become a matter of reclamation. Wearing a dress doesn't change the way I think about what's beautiful, and it doesn't make my ideals less feminist than they were the day before. I'm happy, now, to hike up that long skirt and show everyone that I still don't shave my legs.

I try not to think about what other people wear and what that says about who they are and what they believe. I believe we have the right to wear what we want, and I see "hip" as context-specific. At the Gap, I might be hip in jeans and a $50 sweater, but at an Ani DiFranco concert, I'm more hip with a shaved head. It's a question of whether or not those clothes are an outward expression of what someone believes and whether or not we're in a context where we need that outward expression. No one in our class has to walk around with a button that says "Well-behaved women rarely make history" (a great quote) for us to know she is a feminist.

This is the response we got from Julie.

I loved your post, Teryn.

Zoé, I guess I make a distinction between undergrads and graduate students. I feel more comfortable socializing with grad students, who are more mature and able to process blurred teacher/student boundaries; I also regard graduate students more as colleagues than as students.

After this I kept thinking of all the contradictions, everything that shattered the standards in the class. Julie is way too fashionable to be a feminist. Her hair is a little past her neck in layers and high-lights. She sometimes wears skirts and high boots. Yet she constantly talks about her "partner." Oh, she must be a feminist/lesbian. Then she talks about her partner, *Rob*. Okay, she's a feminist, but she doesn't dress like a man, or smell like patchouli, or act like a lesbian. Talk about disruptive pedagogy.

The class continued, and I kept having to deal with not becoming too close to her, constantly trying to disrupt what the lines of a traditional teacher or student should be. I found myself feeling angry and hurt the last couple of classes, to the point where I felt I was pouting and I wanted to avoid participating in the class. I felt a sense of loss. Somehow the seven of us had managed to create a collective village, where I had, for the first time, been able to establish myself and my unique knowledge. Again, it felt childish to have such feelings of anger, and more so, that I found myself directing that anger toward Julie. Again, I was trying to place her in that mothering role. I was angry at her for making me leave the family unit.

Luckily, I didn't suffer much and was able to find a whole new community when the spring semester began and I enrolled in her "Rhetorics of Scholarship" class. Some of the students in this class were workshopping papers begun in "Feminist Composition." Tensions were high when Jason [aka Devon], the one man in class, greeted a classmate from last semester and her colleague, with whom he had had somewhat hostile confrontations over feminist ideals. He was imposing on the comfort level of the room, in keeping with his physical stature. He was at least 6 feet tall and weighed about 200 pounds; he overshadowed most of us, including Julie's small frame.

The tension was heavy. And for a greet-and-meet exercise, Julie had us write about our ideas and then go around the room and share them. The tension in the room came to a climax when Julie said, "Jason, I am very interested in what you have to say, because I noticed you weren't engaged while we were doing the exercise."

My jaw dropped. I wonder if it was obvious. Julie was obviously using confrontational pedagogy. And again, I regretted the reaction I had had when a woman presented herself in a "manly" assertive fashion in class. "Julie is such a bitch." Of course, I was smart enough to question my own reaction. I knew that if it had been a man who had said what Julie did, I would have seen him as strict and probably would have gotten the impression that this was going to be a class I was going to have to work hard in.

Jason said he wasn't sure if he was going to keep the class, but Julie still asked him to present his ideas. When he started talking about [his research project on] grammar, I let out a disinterested "ugh."

I was sitting next to Julie, so she was able to hear my grunt. She made an example of it by telling the class my reaction was not the reaction one wanted from readers, and then she began discussing issues of rhetoric. In the back of my head I was somewhat frightened. This was a side of Julie I had never seen before. She was being so rude: picking on the one male; using my disinterest in grammar as an example. I didn't know how to gauge the situation, but I imagined this class was going to be different, a lot different than the one before. Needless to say, we sat through an uncomfortable class, in which Julie took the reins and did most of the talking. Jason did not return to class, to my relief.

Again we began to build a community where everyone felt comfortable expressing their ideas, criticizing, etc. At the beginning of the semester Julie had said she would be focusing on her bitch pedagogy. Yet when I came to class late, instead of getting the bitchy reaction I expected, she said,

"That's okay. I know you work."

"Actually, I take off work early on Mondays. I thought you were doing bitch pedagogy this semester."

"Oh, well, in that case, don't do it again." She didn't sound stern but more like my-friend-Julie trying to imitate an "authority figure."

But beyond the confrontation with Jason, Julie also made a stern confrontation to the class. The day the class workshopped my paper Julie turned to me and said, "I guess we're all wondering what's going on." My email had been down during the weekend and no one had received my paper. Furthermore, I had gotten an email from Julie earlier in the week that said something along the lines of, "Zoé, I haven't received your paper. If you want me to give you thorough feedback, I'll need to have it before the weekend; if not, I'll only be able to give you a few suggestions on Monday."

I wrote back, "That's okay. I'm just not ready to share it."

Looking back, I can see how Julie might have felt that I didn't see her comments as valuable. In class, I was distraught. During break, I made copies of my draft. The group hurriedly read it and gave me a couple of minutes of feedback. I did not get a round of applause at the end.

Because of my mistake, the class would be getting out an hour early. But instead of dismissing us, Julie started to ask us questions about what we considered feminist pedagogy and what we didn't like about the traditional classroom. We said we disliked the teacher-focused classroom where there were lectures, quizzes, and we did not have the ability to express our views. Julie then spoke of how, whenever she tried to break from the mold, students tried to force her back into it. She said her expertise was not being valued. And she pretty much made the statement that we did not value her as a teacher or as a human being.

I sat silently through most of the session. I felt as if it were a personal attack. This is not how I would expect Julie to bring up such a subject. It was confrontational much in the way that my mother tries to lay on guilt trips. I was hurt, and I actually felt like Julie was contradicting herself. At the beginning of the semester, we had established that everyone's thoughts were weighed equally, not just hers; now she was upset because we had not regarded her as a serious authority figure.

The class let out. I cried all the way home.

The following class period the same situation happened to another classmate—her computer had died and she had asked her friend to send out her paper; unfortunately her friend sent out the wrong version. Once the class discovered the mistake, Julie made copies for everyone. Feedback was allowed to be given late through email. I picked up my stuff and left as soon as I could. As I was walking down the hall, I heard loud clapping from the group.

I felt like the black sheep.

I can question myself and ask why I had not been confrontational when this tension grew within the class. Looking back on it, I think it had to do with the same confrontational style that Julie took on. To me, she did not fall into the "bitch" category when she was talking to the class. In my eyes she became the "mother." This was my mother telling me how disappointed she was at my efforts. I've had many conversations with my mother where she's told me how I have hurt her. I have never had the ability to stand up to my mother in a verbal confrontation. Seeing my mother reflected in Julie made me shy away from even mentioning my feelings. Just as I had done with female mentors in the past (and as an angry teenager with my mother), I wanted to shut Julie from my life. But I felt I had grown too much to do that to her—and mainly to myself.

The confrontational pedagogy that Julie brought into the class was more than just some theory from a book. It seriously encompassed the whole premise of the class from the way she lectured and facilitated discussions to the way she dressed and the "bitchy" way in which she sometimes dealt with the issues of the class.

I'm not going to lie—as a student it confused me, upset me, frustrated me, and scared me—but this was all taking place in a comfortable environment. By the end of the semester I was trying to disrupt my own ideas, processes, and roles that I play. But again, binary breakdowns can only happen in certain situations, when the instructor is willing to give up the power and the students are willing to step up in the class as individual thinkers and not just as students.

Even with all the new aspects I learned about myself in this class (which were mainly to question the norm), I still find myself slipping back into the binaries. I want my female professors to mother me. I concede to the subordinate student role in classes where I have confrontational males. The main thing I can exercise beyond the class is simply to question the beliefs that I used to maintain as facts. But without continually having a solid community in which to actively voice and question binaries, I fear that, as with any other talent, either you use it or lose it.

A Classroom Space Revisited

By listening rhetorically to the multivoiced, multigenre reconstruction of that troubled classroom space, I hope to reenter it in order to hear what it has to teach me more fully. The first commonality I observe among the juxtaposed narratives is our collective tendency to "slip back into binaries"—to celebrate something called feminist pedagogy, which exists as the laudatory other to the demonized patriarchal (or traditional) pedagogy. This binary, I now realize, has had an enormous impact on the ways I conceive of my pedagogy, despite the fact that disrupting binaries is one of my most often-stated goals. Its tenacity, I believe, resides in the profound disgust I feel toward those teachers who disrespect their students and devalue their situated knowledges and experiences. I so much do not want to be like them that I force myself to occupy a fixed and idealized position as Feminist Teacher. But because there is no such stable thing, I continually feel as if I'm failing—and, too, that my students are letting me down.

Interestingly, this language of betrayal, which reminds me of Zoé's feelings of anger and loss over being forced to leave "the family unit," helps me locate another commonality between us: the problem of forging an identity while occupying a space from which one feels excluded. In *Performing Pedagogy: Toward an Art of Politics,* performance artist and teacher Charles R. Garoian argues that those "who reside on the borders of cultures continually struggle with problems of identity" (163). This insight is not new to me, but it takes on a different significance when I situate it within my experiences as an interdisciplinary scholar of rhetoric and writing and as a teacher committed to forging connections across and beyond the English department. Although I eagerly position myself at the borders of disciplines, genres, and ideologies, for I am convinced that doing so affords considerable revisionary potential, I nevertheless long for a sense of "finishedness," a kind of final answer to that existential question: Who am I? Before my experiences with this graduate class, I thought I had the answer: I am a Feminist Teacher. Furthermore, because most of the students in the course identified as feminists, I expected that I would be able to practice—for the very first time ever—that pedagogy with seamless ease. This expectation that all of us *already understood and agreed upon* what it means to teach and learn as feminists was, ironically, the very sort of aprocess, acontextual quality we had assigned to those unenlightened patriarchal pedagogues.

And yet, as Zoé's reflection makes clear, not all of the students in the course *did* identify as feminists. Indeed, for Zoé herself, the terms of belonging to such a community were so muddled and contradictory that she was moved to question them in webboard posting titled, aptly enough, "A Problematic Class." In the post, Zoé asks two questions, the first of which illustrates her struggle to contend with feminist stereotypes: Is it possible to be fashionable and a feminist? This question garners a lengthy response from Teryn about the need to contextualize "hipness" and to question standards of beauty. In my subsequent post, I praise Teryn's insights, telling her that I "love" what she wrote. My zealous praise, when coupled with my somewhat dismissive response to Zoé's post, reinforced, I believe, Zoé's feelings of being the course "black sheep," the student newest to feminism, the one who did not quite belong. Furthermore, by focusing my attention on Teryn's response to Zoé's *first* question, I was able to conveniently ignore the second: Would this class be as successful if we had a professor with a different personality or teaching style? This second question, which emerges for me now as a critically intervening one, is troubling because it demands that I interrogate feminist pedagogy in relation to a particular "style" or "personality," the very problem I sought to avoid by assuming the idealized position of Feminist Teacher. Rather than contend with this question and the discomfort it generated for me, I ignored it completely, preferring instead to align myself with Teryn's post and the confident version of feminism it offered me.

Now, however, when I consider Zoé's second question seriously, I wonder: What personality/style did I perform in Feminist Composition that made Zoé declare it (but not Rhetorics of Scholarship) a "success"? I know I leaned more toward the "nurturing mother" style in that first course. Motivated to perform a different version of feminist pedagogy in the second, I tried to practice a confrontational style, which bell hooks explains as

> a model of pedagogy that is based on the assumption that many students will take courses from me who are afraid to assert themselves as critical thinkers, who are afraid to speak (especially students from oppressed and exploited groups). The revolutionary hope that I bring to the classroom is that it will become a space where they can come to voice. Unlike the stereotypical feminist model that suggests women can best come to voice in an atmosphere of safety (one in which we are all going to be kind and nurturing), I encourage students to work at coming to voice in an atmosphere where they might be afraid or see themselves as at risk. The goal is to enable all students, not just an assertive few, to feel empowered in a rigorous, critical discussion. ("Toward," 53)

Similarly, Ronald Strickland argues that teachers who want their students to learn to resist dominant ideologies must practice a confrontational pedagogy, one that acknowledges rather than ignores or represses conflicts. Such a pedagogy, he contends, "open[s] up the classroom for productive contestation and interrogation of existing paradigms of knowledge (as opposed to the mere reproduction of knowledge, or the transmission of information as knowledge)" (292). As I designed the Rhetorics of Scholarship course, hooks's and Strickland's descriptions of a nontraditional, confrontational pedagogy appealed to me, both because I wanted my students to resist dominant ideologies about what should "count" as academic scholarship and because I felt I had been too "stereotypically nurturing" the previous term.

My students' narratives, however, disrupt the nurturing mother/ confrontational bitch binary, exposing how one person's confrontation can be another person's experience of motherly love. Marie, for example, celebrates my decision to confront Devon on his refusal to freewrite, observing that she admired and felt empowered by my decision—very different feelings, I'm sure, from those experienced by Devon.[1] Marie's reflections on this classroom moment also help me understand my reasons for risking it; that is, my strongest motivation for confronting Devon was to protect and nurture the community we were just beginning to form. Consequently, I was never really "free" of that motherly impulse, despite my intentions to act otherwise.

Zoé's reaction to the second moment of confrontation also problematizes a mother/bitch binary. To recall, Zoé experienced my comments as a "personal attack," an attempt to "guilt trip" her and the other students in class for disappointing me. By interpreting my remarks in this way, Zoé experiences me not as the confrontational pedagogue attempting to communicate strategies of resistance but rather as *her own mother,* someone she reports she "never had the ability to stand up to" in verbal disagreements.

Listening rhetorically to these collected reflective narratives is a first step toward dismantling a pedagogical pendulum that has been influencing me for years: When I'm too much mother one term, I compensate by being full-fledged bitch the next. Pushed to locate myself beyond this binary, I now look for new ways to identify as a feminist teacher of writing. I realize now, for example, that the subject positions I describe earlier in my narrative are subjectivities I *choose,* not fixed identities that plague feminist teachers everywhere. And, by naming them as I do, I can begin to see why I choose them. Most significantly, they simultaneously validate (The Injured Party, The Dummy, The New Prof/Orphaned Grad Student); romanticize (The Process Goddess, The Equalizer); and assuage (The Hard Ass, The Martyr), those feelings of disrespect and worthlessness that are no doubt vestiges from my upbringing and over thirty years of gendered female experience, but are also, I believe, the consequence of being disciplined as a feminist and a RhetComp scholar—two identifying contexts that found their emergent energies through oppositional definition against larger, more oppressive groups. In other words, these subject positions help to keep me feeling marginalized, help me *want* to continue feeling marginalized, and, when I no longer want to feel that way, help me blame others for feeling as I do. In reference to this last point, The Envyist serves the useful function of allowing me to continue stereotyping senior male literature professors and thereby avoid initiating conversations with them about how they teach and why.

Toward a Revisionary Theory of Teaching

I am not naïve enough to think that listing these subjectivities will purge me of them, nor do I necessarily want to rid myself of them. I have come to love and depend on some of them as treasured friends, especially The Hard Ass. But I do believe that naming them, giving them characters and personalities, can help me play with them in ways that might alleviate their unconscious influence in my classrooms and research. By identifying them and the pedagogical genres they inspire, I can rhetorically choose from among them rather than unconsciously summon them.[2]

   The knowledge that pedagogical performance is a rhetorical choice rather than the "natural" consequence of identity (Feminist Teacher) challenges universalist claims about how feminists and other oppositional teachers "should" teach.[3] Rather than begin with claims to identity, a strategy that repeatedly offered me nothing but binary options, I can instead foreground my feminist-motivated pedagogical *purpose*—to teach students the revisionary potential of disruption and delayed community. With this goal in mind, I can redefine teaching "styles"—i.e., nurturing, traditional, and confrontational—as performance genres and generate disruption by self-consciously juxtaposing them within the classroom space. In so doing, I can begin to explore with my students how their identities as thinkers and learners are constructed in response to them. I am curious to understand, for example, how students who are overly comfortable with the genre of teacher-led discussion might be productively disorientated in classroom spaces where teachers self-consciously migrate to solitary writing activities and then to student-led discussions. I wonder, too, how Zoé might have benefited from processing with the class her reactions to my changing pedagogical performances. For example, when I "imitated" the style of a traditional authority and "ordered" her to get to class on time, Zoé did not assume the position of student-child, for she constructed me as neither nurturing mother nor feared father. Instead, she recognized that I was playing a role, and the spirit of serious play with which such performances are undertaken can go a long way toward making the pain of revision bearable.

Just as multigenre texts can generate a productive discomfort necessary to question and revise, so too can multigenre pedagogies help construct classroom spaces where students and teachers can identify, question, play with, and revise their identities. In his descriptions of classroom performance exercises, Charles Garoian suggests some ways both students and teachers might migrate to pedagogical genres previously labeled by many feminist and writing teachers as being "off limits." Students in his art history classes, for example, lecture on specific topics, but they are asked to deliver their research in forms that problematize it, that expose its contradictions and limitations. In response to this assignment, one student delivered a lecture on existentialist art while walking on a treadmill, which functioned as a "visual and conceptual metaphor to represent 'futility' in existentialism and in daily life" (30). By juxtaposing her lecture with a mode of delivery that questioned the everyday value of its content, Garoian's student models a method of lecturing that need not be a patriarchal dissemination of information; rather, we can revise what a lecture might mean—an invitation to listeners to question and challenge content *as it is being delivered*. Although this is something we might already expect graduate students will do, my experiences have taught me that banking methods of learning are so entrenched (and easier) that students at both the graduate and undergraduate levels need teachers to disrupt their conditioning in obvious and direct ways.

Furthermore, as Lori Alden Ostergaard argues in a performative webtext, such self-conscious deployments of rhetoric's fifth canon can also foreground the ways in which silenced power differentials authorize and regulate the blending of speech and movement in classroom spaces. The animated delivery of women, for example, is more frequently interpreted as being irrational and/or hysterical in contrast to similar deliveries made by men. To understand how the delivery of different pedagogical genres is tied both to genre and the physical body of its speaker, teachers and students might reflect on and discuss whose and which kinds of performances disturb them the most, make them the most physically uncomfortable, and why.

Finally, by lecturing in the performative manner Garoian and Ostergaard advocate, I can acknowledge and affirm the needs of The Dummy, The New Prof/Orphaned Grad Student, and The Envyist. In other words, it *is* possible for me to demonstrate my knowledge and expertise in forms that do not undermine my feminist commitments. And although ideally I would possess the self-worth necessary to avoid feeling the need to make such demonstrations, I cannot say as yet that I do.

Which brings me, then, to the issue of confidence, a term Aristotle defines as the opposite of fear. His binary challenges yet another I have been unconsciously working with and struggling against for a long time, namely, that fear's opposite is not confidence but rather safety. For years I have been laboring to create classrooms where students feel safe, believing that fear's presence will prevent them from doing their best and hardest work. What I'm coming to realize is that safety is a murky term, one obscured by too much easy expectation: We'll be safe if we keep our doors locked or if we hunker down against those grueling pangs of loneliness and limit our talk with strangers. These notions of safety, however, are premised on a concept of avoidance; they lack the urgency that is sometimes necessary if we are to create spaces where people feel able to say the hardest things. It is in this way that the capacity to confront is a necessary condition for the construction of confidence-inspiring classrooms. When I say "confront," I do not mean the kind of dismissive angry gesture I've railed against throughout this book, though surely such ammunition has its rhetorical purposes. Nor do I mean agonistic discourse in the sense of Socratic dialogue, where speakers' abilities to make Swiss cheese out of seemingly solid logical arguments determine their rhetorical prowess. Instead, I have in mind a kind of face-to-face talk where confrontation is the clear and direct expression of something a listener more than likely does not want to hear but *needs* to hear if members of a discursive community are to continue in their willingness to listen to and learn from one another.

Such a pedagogy will surely frighten students and teachers alike. I remember what Devon said when I asked him to share with the class his concerns about our seminar: "That's not something I could ever do." In that moment, I believe my pedagogy was, for him, scary and unsafe. After all, he elected to drop the class, and maybe I was asking for too much too soon. I don't know. Despite this uncertainty, however, or perhaps because of it, I am beginning to believe that a certain kind of fear—one that galvanizes confidence—may have its place in my classroom after all.

Epilogue
On Lack, Progress, and Perfection

Every semester at least a handful of students writes that their goal for the course is to learn how to write the "perfect" paper. My recovering good-girl, the one who always felt pressure to be perfect, who learned early not to speak or act or move unless she knew she was right, cringes. I worry: How can I help these students revise, to take risks and get messy with their language and their thinking, if they're so hung up on perfection? How can I help them understand that writing doesn't lead to perfect Truth, that it simply leads to more writing?

When revision and feminism meet, we are obligated to examine the concept of progression: the belief that with hard work, tomorrow's version can be better than today's. As I have worked on this book, I have struggled with the tension this key term creates. That is, as a writing teacher, I *do* believe that students' drafts can and should improve over time. As a feminist, I *need* to believe that society can change for the better. But as a writer who identifies with postmodernist thought, I do not want to buy into the myth of linear progression, the belief that history can be written as a story of continuous improvement. In my process of writing this book, I have done, I'm sure, what many of my students do when their beliefs, needs, and theories create seemingly unresolvable tensions: I have ignored them. As one part of me repeated, "you need to deal with progression, Julie," the other part, the louder part, kept answering, "yeah, okay, but later. Later."

When later arrived and I finally braved Foucault, looking for passages where he trashes the concept of progression, you can imagine my relief when I discovered I had misread him. In fact, in a passage that seems written to me personally, Foucault explains:

> I don't say that humanity doesn't progress. I say that is it a
> bad method to pose the problem as: "How is that we have
> progressed?" The problem is: how do things happen? And
> what happens now is not necessarily better or more ad-
> vanced, or better understood, than what happened in the
> past. (50)

When we study our past assuming that it has improved, we fail to
see and therefore be held accountable for the histories of our regres-
sion, those instances when we behaved badly, when we ignored the
suffering of others, or perhaps when we caused such suffering ourselves. A progressivist method thus leads us to abandon these instances in favor of a story line that makes us look better, but it also,
ultimately, fails to help us understand ourselves *as we really are*. It
is this ability to see ourselves truthfully, flaws and all, that is necessary for humanity to progress.

As a forward-looking gesture, *progression* is committed to understanding the present so that the future might improve. Such a
gesture also recognizes that there is something lacking in the present
that must be contended with if our drafts and our lives are going to
progress. Typically, from our students' perspectives, this something
"lacking" is considered an absence that if only they had access to
their teachers' minds and preferences they could fill and all would
be well. Instead of theorizing lack as a flawed absence, I want to
think of it as an unheard and potentially transformative presence,
something that is already in the draft but is currently and unconsciously being ignored. Such a theorizing of lack gets our students
away from rereading their drafts from the position of always already
failed writer, a belief that, according to Donald Murray ("Internal"),
leads many writers to associate revision with the shame-based feeling of "having" to rewrite.

The French feminists, of course, have modeled for us the revisionary potential of theorizing repressed presence. When confronted
with theories of psychosexual development that position woman as
always already lacking, as incapable of accessing the symbolic order

except through relationships with men, they responded with écriture feminine, a language of woman that

> reverses the hierarchy of male and female sexuality . . . by enunciating woman's sexual embodiment as the general model of sexuality and showing male sexuality as a variant of it. . . . [I]nstead of lack, woman's body is oversupplied. . . . Woman's sexuality is not one, but two, or even plural, the multiplicity of sexualized zones spread across the body. (Dallery, 290–91)

They thus revise "woman-as-lack" into theories of women's language that serve "as a constant, repressed threat to the patriarchal symbolic order" (Weedon, 55). The French feminists' revisions thereby expose that what is lacking is not "woman" at all but rather the patriarchal psychoanalytic theories that ignore the fullness of a sexuality that threatens them.

By attending to the unheard presences in our texts and in our lives, we have the means to make them more whole. Expressing her understanding of perfection-as-wholeness, Nancy Mairs writes:

> I really did, and do, believe that my life is perfect, although I recognize that certain details of it—like my own advancing debilitation by multiple sclerosis and my husband's metastatic melanoma—might seem from the outside to forbid it such status. . . . The truth is . . . that although "perfect" may mean "flawless," it may mean "consummate" or "whole" as well, and it is in this sense that I cherish my life as I could not, perhaps, without its flaws. (*Voice*, 1–2)

Becoming more whole means being willing to embrace what we would sooner not have to, the "lacks" of our texts and our lives. It means being willing to resee the negativity of our experience in ways that transform our futures.

When I am asked to talk with students about revision, I always start by reading the above passage and then asking them to think about the lab reports they've written in science classes. I remind them of how, when plotting data on the x-y plane, they are instructed to draw the best-fit curve, the line that best approximates the movement of the experiment. Because the line is an approximation, it comes near to but does not intersect most of the charted data points. As students in science classes, we learn that this approximation is the best thing going. We are told that had we done the experiments perfectly, if we'd performed them in a sealed vacuum, let's say, or if we'd stopped breathing long enough to keep our hand from shaking, then there would be no error, and there would be no need to approximate. (Mathematicians call this sort of reasoning "hand-waving." We know we're human, after all, so let's work with what we've got and see what happens.) Most of the students I talk with nod their heads knowingly; some of them have just come from classes where they have had to write these kinds of reports. Relying on our shared ethos as struggling scientific writers, I remind them of when, in almost all scientific experiments, one point inevitably falls outside the approximated curve. In fact, this point falls so far outside the best-fit curve that if we were to include it we would no longer have a curve at all. So we are told to ignore it. We are told that the point is an anomaly. Maybe we tripped while pouring the beaker. Perhaps we started our measurements with the wrong end of the ruler. Whatever the reason, our egregious human error necessitates that the point, for the sake of the whole, be ignored.

This is the very point, of course, that in writing, while revising, we are obligated to follow. We must follow it closely and carefully until our texts as we know them fall apart and we are thereby authorized to begin again. I tell my students to look for this point in their conclusions. "What's there that doesn't seem to fit?" I ask. "What are you tempted to cut?" Or I tell them to reread their drafts, looking for passages they've already scratched out for the sake of some obvious but limited whole. I explain to them that revising requires us to pay attention to the ideas and passages we wish we could ignore. I tell them that when we can hold off long enough to allow our papers to fall apart, they become more whole.

When my students look at me oddly, I smile and try again. I ask them to think of a time when they saw a person they thought they knew well change when encountered in a radically different context. "The person didn't become more perfect," I explain. "But he or she did become more whole, for you, in your eyes." I describe a few such moments from my own life, such as when I heard William F. Buckley play jazz piano like a monster. Or the time at my friend Barry's funeral, when one of his former students, an ex-con, talked about what Barry had meant to him. I tell them about how so often we only experience each other, and ourselves, as the tip of an iceberg, and if we can, through our revising—and before our funerals—help each other become more whole, we are doing something that matters. We are, in fact, progressing toward perfection.

When I teach revision, I strive to make the Derridean deconstructive project a reconstructive one as well—a process wherein a writer realizes that her current draft contains all it ever needs for perfection. Now begins the lifelong task of rereading it in order to hear those silent presences that will make it more whole.

Price Hill, circa Nineteen-Sixty-Something

In my favorite family
photograph, I am absent. The women
a mother, her mother
stand in front, arms flung around four
proud toddlers, the oldest holds
a basket of pastel eggs. There's a sense
they've just come from Mass and soon
will go indoors for Cokes in small
nonreturnable bottles.

In the second row is an alcoholic who once owned a bar
in the flood zones of Cincinnati. His life had a kind of
    symmetry

I can appreciate. During a hold-up that didn't amount to much
(he hid the big bills in his shoe) he was shot in the leg. I
  know
this because I've read the yellowed newspaper clipping.
  That year
I retreated often to read up on my family history.
As the story goes, my mother's version of the story,
my grandfather the alcoholic bartender
who knew a thousand dirty jokes but shared only the clean
drank because he was plagued by daily headaches.

In the final row
twice removed from the toddlers and the eggs
stands my father. He's in suit pants, a white-collared shirt, a
  tie.
He has his hands on his hips, and he's wearing the familiar
  wiry glasses
I've come to associate with all his early photos:
slightly cross-eyed, refusing to pose.
Years later I guess right: five kids by 30.
It all happened so fast.

A stone garden makes itself against
an exterior wall. I am curious.
Is my mother pregnant with me
or is that just the wind picking up the fullness of her Sunday
  dress?

In my version of the story, I am not yet born
though surely my brother looks older than two.
I am expectation and hope, holding
out for connection and two-dimensional space.
Or maybe I'm upstairs napping in a crib
that's been slept in for years. No one
is minding me. When stirred like the moon
I stand and disclose my interior

A periodic witness
resurrected whole.

In her summary of the postmodern project, Jane Flax explains how

> postmodernists construct stories about the Enlightenment
> in which the disparate views of a variety of thinkers, includ-
> ing Descartes, Kant, and Hegel, are integrated into (and
> reduced to) one "master narrative." This master narrative
> then serves as an adversary against which postmodernist
> rhetoric can be deployed. (30)

As someone trained in rhetoric, I am not surprised by this move to create a common enemy to work against. I have done it often enough myself. But now, as I write this epilogue and reread Flax's passage, "disparate" and "reduced to" emerge for me with more pressing importance. I realize that in constructing my opposition, I inevitably reduce its complexity. I engage in what I call synecdochic understanding, using part of something to represent the whole. I have, for example, read about postmodern theory, but I have not read enough Descartes, Kant, and Hegel to understand how and why their views conflict. Instead, I have joined the rush to group them together as thinkers whose shared belief in a "rationalist and teleological philosophy of history" (Flax, 31) mark them as ironically unenlightened. It is in this sense that a rush to convergence is most troubling to me: when our rush to establish our own authority denies the wholeness of others.

We can't read everything, of course. And our language theories tell us that we will always leave something out, even when our intention is to say it all. Yet, there are, as I hope this book as demonstrated, strategies for writing that make reductive convergence difficult. For example, I invite you to summarize cleanly this epilogue for someone who has not read it. Can you do it? If not, is that because it is poorly written or poorly read?

Let's try something else entirely. Let's say I wrote it like this because I want to show you how texts that contain obvious pockets of silence create gaps out of which you can respond. And, too, I wrote it like this because I *want* you to respond, to make connections with me, ones I have not yet made. Most important, I wrote it like this because I want you to feel invited into this discourse in such a way that you cannot write about me and my work without being conscious of your own tendency to reduce it, to latch on to some part of it, and to use that part to represent its whole.

In May I attend a Buddhist service led by a monk visiting from Tibet. The space is filled with colorful murals, offering bowls, many different kinds of people—some in long flowing dresses, some in shorts and T-shirts. It's already hot, and I am nervous. This is only my third time. I don't wait long before we rise in silence. We clear the aisle for our visitor, who is quickly surrounded by adoring faces, most of them bowed. He walks slowly, shaved head bowed in return, a small smile on his aging face. When he speaks, he is hard to understand. I try to hold on to the rhythms of his English. He tells me to be patient, to pick up what seems to make sense, and to give up the belief that I must remember everything he teaches today for me to benefit from spiritual practice.

"Think of these lectures as Dharma flea markets," he jokes. "Pick up what you like for now and come back for more later."

Today he teaches me about humility.

Cut poems in chapter four—not good enough.
—from revision notes, 12/02/01

Homecoming

South of the Ohio suburb
where I spent winter days
tubing ice ramps down
the hill out back
and summer nights chasing

lightning bugs and storing them in glass
jars with punctured lids

where I once cut down
my older brother
who at the age of twelve decided to hang
himself from the tree out front
close enough to the street to earn
the neighbors' attentions
deep enough for my mother's
he's just looking for attention

south of that suburb is another suburb
which we used to call the boondocks and is now plotted
with homes sporting an architecture bordering
on the grotesque, angular and huge,
too few windows and identical decks.
Where is the light supposed to go?

I'm sitting in my mother's Oldsmobile.
We just bought corn from a roadside stand.
We're passing streets named
Cobblestone Crossing Court and Tifton Green Trail.
North of here is where I grew up.

Later I'll ride bikes with my brother
through these same streets and we'll hear
a concert in the park. He'll eat a hot dog
and a soft pretzel with salt and no mustard
and I'll notice how knee-length denim jeans
seem to be all the rage.
We won't talk much and when the concert dies
down we'll ride home
he in the lead, like he's always been,
silently pointing out bumps in the sidewalk

taking short cuts I don't notice
daring me to go faster than I dare.
I'll remember how we
after dinner at dusk at just this time of night
used to chase lightening bugs
plot their path in space and always guess wrong
catch them in our hands
and let them go.

During the ride home
through the mill parking lot
past Friendly's Ice Cream Shoppe
and the Seventh Adventist Church
I'll understand what homecoming means.

He's got a job he hates and a mortgage to pay.
I can't seem to make him laugh like I used to.
Somewhere between that suburb and this one
we became ordinary.

I suppose a more encompassing version of revision recognizes that we must also accept things as they are, people for who they are. We have to accept this because, in the end, when the paper is handed in or the history is written or the relationship falls apart, we have to be held accountable.

My scene begins with a rhetorical triangle. There is someone saying something to someone else, and what is being said is said in a particular time and place, for particular reasons. There is a writer's effort to be believed and a reader's need to be appreciated. There is reasoning and, one can hope, passion. When it is over, there is satisfaction, persuasion, belief.

The curtain falls, and another triangle takes the stage, one where the three vertices of hope, help, and purpose are wrapped in an awareness provoked by pain.

If writing is a process of making room for love, and I believe that it is, then what I have learned—through this writing, through my students, my teachers, myself—is that revision is a process of making room for pain.

Appendixes

Notes

Works Cited

Index

Appendix A
English 300 Seminar Project

Brief Review (from your syllabus)
Due at the time of the scheduled final exam, your *Seminar Project* represents the conceptual (rather than material) culmination of your work as an English major. In it you will situate selected texts you've already produced within an interpretive framework—an introductory essay and a concluding essay—that makes personal, institutional, and theoretical (dis)connections across them.

Some Specifics
You are required to produce at least fifteen pages of new prose; students who earn an A will produce at least twenty pages. As we discussed in class, you can divide this requirement in half, using eight or so pages for your introduction and eight for your conclusion. You can also divide the requirement into smaller sections, although be advised that it can be difficult to develop the level of theoretical and reflective complexity I'm expecting in shorter pieces.

Tips
Gather all the writing you have produced as an English major in a department committed to an English studies model and make (dis)connections across those texts. Analyze how you are writing, how you are presenting yourself as a writer and a thinker in each of the pieces. Then explore why any differences and similarities exist. What can these (dis)connections teach us about the nature of English studies? What kind of student is this department producing, as evidenced by your published work? Is this good or bad? Why?

While making these connections, avoid remaining at the level of description (i.e., "I analyzed short stories in my prose class and poems in my poetry class"). Instead, *you need to ask and offer tentative answers to HOW and WHY questions:* How did you think and write for each class? Why? What kind of work did each course value, and why (reread old syllabi for clues)? How did the ideologies and assumptions upon which each course was founded affect what, how, and why you read and wrote? These are the more complex kinds of questions you need to be asking and answering.

You're also invited to make the same kinds of (dis)connections between the texts you produced in school with those that provide evidence of your life outside of school. Again, go beyond the merely descriptive and into the theoretical and reflective. For example, if one of your outside texts represents your deep religious convictions, you can analyze how your religious ideologies challenged some of the interpretive theories you may have been exposed to in your English classes. How, for example, did you deal with the postmodern assertion that there is no one Truth? How did you integrate the competing theories and ideologies in your life? Or did you? How do you see your out-of-school ideologies affecting the choices you made as an English major (e.g., the kinds of courses you avoided, selected; the kinds of texts you read; the kinds of readings and interpretations you produced). By making these types of (dis)connections, you'll be theorizing how English majors are not created in a vacuum; instead, they are the product of the many competing discourses that shape a life.

Look to Alice Walker's *The Same River Twice* for an example of how to structure new prose around representative life/school texts. Notice that she includes a lot of texts written by people other than herself (letters from friends, articles and columns written by critics, photographs, etc.) to create a context for each chapter. You can do the same sort of thing to illustrate how the discourses you've encountered and contended with were not always (and were not often) the ones you wrote.

Appendix B
Rereading Process Used in Revision of Early Draft of Chapter 4, "Toward Hearing the Impossible"

To examine how an ultimate perspective is arrived at in my own multigenre revision of Robert Connors's essay, I reread and reflect on an early rough draft of my essay, "Toward Hearing the Impossible." (This rereading process prompted revisions that ultimately resulted in the chapter 4 of this book.) I begin by recognizing the various positions of the voices speaking throughout. My voice as researcher opens the essay, contextualizing the interviewees' responses and explaining that my hope is "to give voice to the emotional silences in Connors's essay." The next voice belongs to John, who speaks a few of these silences as he explains how his own troubled relationship with his father caused him, as a student, to distrust male mentor figures and how he sees this same distrust, which takes form in the refusal to listen, existing within his own male students. Scott's voice follows, with a rambling discussion of what he perceives to be Connors's simultaneous sincerity as a writing teacher and his inadequacies as a feminist theorist. While he takes issue with some of Connors's generalizations regarding male and female students, he does agree that male teachers and students disconnect on what he terms "the testosterone level" and that these disconnections make it difficult to discuss "effeminate" subjects such as poetry. Todd then steps forward and gives voice to his discomfort with Connors's assumption that mentoring *ought to* be written into the curriculum. He is suspicious of this type of "touchy-feely" maneuvering and argues on the basis of personal experience that the best mentoring relationships are founded on academic—not emotional—connections and that these sorts of relationships emerge naturally within the context of an academic course.

The essay breaks, and I emerge not as researcher but instead as a woman at home alone, writing in her journal and marveling at the "respect and seriousness" with which the men treated her work. I feel touched by their willingness to open up to me, and I write of my connection with John and the sadness I felt over our shared experiences of growing up with inaccessible, absent fathers. Another space break follows, and John returns, this time speaking of his reluctance to mentor male students because he doesn't have enough time. Tony then speaks for the first time, also giving voice to his discomfort with mentoring male students, how he struggles with the "weight of that responsibility." He speaks touchingly of his relationship with a lonely student from Minnesota who wrote powerful essays about his troubled relationship with an abusive father. Like John, Tony is worried about time and students crossing boundaries in uncomfortable, intrusive ways. Scott follows, with a story about a male student who was "lashing out" in class because he was so terrified of the transition into college. Scott reports that this student needed to be told to "grow up," something Scott-as-teacher feels nervous about having said but nevertheless feels was the right thing to do, as the student "took writing more seriously after we talked."

Following another space break, my journal voice returns, this time speaking of feeling love for Tony's honest revelation of struggle and pain. In the next section, the men reflect on their own relationships with male mentor figures. Scott admits: "I don't like men much" and reports that, while he maintains relationships with former women professors, he feels "no sense of urgency to keep in touch with the guys." Paul then speaks for the first time, reflecting on his complex relationship with his father, who is both enthusiastic mentor and harsh, judgmental critic. I break the narrative line of the essay yet again with a metadiscursive comment regarding my pull toward complicated, messy texts and Paul's observation that this "pull" is about my attraction to men who can't commit.

What follows then is my reflection on a literacy autobiography I wrote while enrolled in a graduate seminar titled "Essentials of Reading and Writing." The piece follows, and although it professes to be about revision and silence, it is also about the embarrassment

I used to feel and often still feel over "exposing secrets" and making myself and my emotions known—both to others and especially to myself. I can write of loneliness and violence only from a removed, detached perspective. The intimacy is limited and temporary. Throughout, there is an absence of feeling, of action, and most profoundly of memory.

I follow my literacy autobiography with another space break and the voices of John, Tony, and Paul, all three of whom describe their yearning and need for male guidance, and the lack of it in their lives. They speak of pain and depression growing up, of finding outlets in sports, drugs, and violence, and of the unmet need that someone recognize and take seriously their unhappiness. I follow this section with a self-authored poem that describes my relationship growing up with a desperately unhappy brother whose pain was largely ignored and how I've since learned that I'm not special anymore, and that perhaps I never was—because pain is ordinary, and it is our failure to acknowledge that fact that fuels despair.

My revision of Connors's essay closes with another metadiscursive comment, which describes what's been happening between me and the male teachers since the interviews concluded. They maintain connection with me by leaving me notes, related articles, essays, and short stories. Other men not initially interviewed begin to seek me out, stopping me in the English department hallway and telling me they'd like to talk, too.

To arrive at a unifying, transcendent term, recall that Burke indicates it usually resides implicitly in the beginning and it is only made explicit after all obscurities are washed away. Because I as researcher have the last word, it is tempting to assume that it is me who makes the term explicit and also to assume that term to be *connection*—more specifically, my *desirability as agent of connection*—a move that would position my voice over those of my collaborators and my other selves by making me "special" again. I resist this term because I no longer want to be the one who saves men in pain by connecting them to the world. While being special enabled me to survive as a child, to connect with a brother whom I so very much needed, it proves to be a dysfunctional term for a woman seeking healthy, intimate relationships with men. So I give up *connection* and reread my revised essay, looking for a transcendent term I can live with.

When I go back to read the beginning of the essay, I realize that the endnote, which includes a copy of the initial memo I sent to male writing teachers asking them to participate in my study, is actually the essay's "beginning," for it is here that my transcendent term takes root. The memo's tone, in its attempt to be rhetorically persuasive, is flirtatious. Although I wasn't conscious of it at the time (I thought I was just being funny), I use sex to appeal to these men, almost all of them single and heterosexual. (Note: In their reflections on conducting ethnographic research on academic men, Judith Newton and Judith Stacey observe a similar effect: "Fieldwork . . . had begun to mimic, perhaps parody, heterosexual dating conventions and to erect surprising constraints on our capacity for critical analysis of the lives and texts of our subject" (297). For example, the "seductiveness of the intimate interview situation in which a rapt, female audience . . . attended appreciatively to the male subjects' every word" (298), led one participant to remark, "'There's an erotic side to this . . . that we aren't talking about, that I'm sure is going to be true of almost all the men that are involved in this issue. . . . That's one of the reasons it's fun to talk to you, and a lot comes out'" (299).) The tone gets more complex when I give the men a list of responses they can "check off," indicating their interest in participating. One such response, which ironically mimics the voice of a man threatened by feminists "like me," reads:

> This is a feminist plot of some sort. You secretly hate that Connors essay and want to trap me somehow. I need to know more before I can ~~commit~~ agree to read and talk about his essay. Call/email me at. . . .

By putting *commit* under erasure, I'm using flirtatious irony to forge a bond with each respondent: We both know that women often "accuse" men of being afraid to commit; we both know that this is especially true of men who equate commitment and "trap." My ironic tone enables me to position myself as something other than an "angry feminist," an identity I worked hard to avoid, as I needed the men to allow me to interview them. Of course, as my initial reading of Connors's essay makes clear (see chapter 4), I was indeed a very angry feminist. Interestingly, only one of the interviewees actually checked this response, but he did so in a way that returned the ironic volley; next to his home phone number he wrote, "'cause every chick should get my number (ha! ha!)" Another respondent wrote, "cute," next to the response, and another called me at home to say my memo was, "fucking hilarious, especially the part about commit."

With commit in mind as a potential transcendent term, I read through the first three male voices in my multigenre revision. Through their interview responses, I see the different ways they strive and struggle to connect with men. For John, his own past difficulties relating to older men facilitates his connection with younger men. For Scott, positioning himself more as a student than a "man of wisdom" in the classroom helps him connect with students who might feel alienated by the course subject matter. For Todd, teacher-student connections are best made in a nonemotional context, one that foregrounds shared academic interests. After reading these passages, I see two new key terms emerging—*struggle* and *connection*—and I wonder how they work with and against the complexities of commit.

Then it hits me. Commit signifies the struggle to forge and maintain connection, even when connection is that which is most desired. I had spent so much time focusing on how these solitary men connected with me during the interviews that I failed to notice the disconnections that were present throughout. For example, while these teachers are moved to connect with their students, they are also made uncomfortable by the expectations and demands of that connection. They worry about time, about becoming too much of a "friend" and not enough of a teacher, about founding a relationship on forced emotion rather than on academic respect. As I track the struggles created by disconnections throughout the piece, I also notice how I recreated those struggles by the way I structured the different voices. Compelling personal stories are juxtaposed with more distanced theorizing about the role of the writing teacher;

worries about not feeling up to the responsibilities of mentoring are followed by moving examples of mentoring-in-progress. And my own voice flows in and out of the interview passages in disconnected ways. I silence my voice as interviewer, but I choose to include myself as journal writer. I realize that while I was obviously deeply moved by the interviewees' expressions of personal honesty, I could not bring myself to tell them in person; instead, I went home and wrote about it in my journal, a "private" place that I felt compelled to make public in the multigenre revision. This move to expose previously private and potentially embarrassing emotion to a re-moved audience, one not intimately involved in the project, paral-lels my decision to include my literacy autobiography, with its child-hood diary entries and memories, as part of the essay but not as part of a letter sent home.

Thus, when ~~commit~~ is tracked throughout my essay, I see how all the research participants both yearn to connect and struggle with the consequences of that connection made real. The structure of the revision matches the rhythms of intimacy. People with whom we desire connection will inevitably separate out, and that separation will bring ordinary pain. The transcendent term, then, revealed by this unified dialogue is *relationship*, which gathers all the others— sex, connection, commitment, struggle, friendship, and pain—under its wing and reminds us that a relational rhetoric cannot sidestep the darkness, no matter how much we might yearn for it to do so.

Notes

Preface

1. Throughout this book, I use the term *identity/ies* when the subject position/s I am describing feel fixed to me (despite my cognitive awareness that they are not). I use the term *subjectivity/ies* in situations where the constructed representation/s feel more fluid and open to revision.

2. Why the "feminist composition" moniker should evoke this construct rather than, say, images of feminists building alliances with one another and thereby flourishing within English departments, is in part due to the disciplining effect of what I refer to as narratives of marginality—tales regaling all manner of contemptuous and unjust treatment dished out by "non-Comp" people toward those committed to researching and teaching writing. These narratives circulate in nearly every institutional space I inhabit: journals and books, conferences, listservs, committee meetings, offices, hallways. I have heard very few—and need to hear more stories about—feminist compositionists who thrive within English departments by building alliances with "non-Comp" colleagues and administrators.

3. I thank Lori Alden Ostergaard for introducing me to this concept.

4. For more on theories of play within rhetoric and composition studies, see Rouzie, as well as Welch, "Playing." For a discussion of arguments that counter the popular dismissal of "play" in education, see Dunn.

1. Writing That Listens: Defining Revisionary Rhetoric

1. Students wrote similar letters to their peers, asking questions that forced a deeper kind of revision.

2. I want to be sure to differentiate between research on writing, official guides to writing, and actual writing practices. For my purposes, I focus here on the ways in which positivistic epistemological theories contributed to the construction of "nonrevisionary" revision pedagogies. However, many writers actually wrote revisionary texts long before the late 1970s. Jean Toomer's multigenre book *Cane*, for example, appeared in 1923. Also, as Jacqueline Jones Royster makes clear in *Traces of a Stream,* nineteenth-century African American women writers recognized the sociopolitical value of the essay form in the simultaneous fights for literacy and human rights. Specifically, she identifies Maria W. Stewart as the first African American woman to publish an essay (1831). Although Stewart did not write multigenre texts per se, which are the

focus of my inquiry, she did publish texts that spanned multiple genres, including pamphlets, public lectures, legal documents, and religious meditations (Royster, 166).

3. In "Feminism and Composition: The Case for Conflict," Susan C. Jarratt argues that teachers committed to a feminist critical pedagogy need to question their unexamined application of expressivist rhetoric, which emphasizes the need for a supportive and caring classroom as a conduit for authentic student writing. By advocating the value of sustaining and examining conflict in feminist contexts, Jarratt lays the groundwork for my specific examination of revision.

4. Feminist scholars working in rhetoric and composition studies have attempted to explain why feminist theories came relatively late to the discipline. Susan Wall, for example, hypothesizes that the influential cognitive studies conducted by women in the discipline (i.e., Flower, Emig, Perl) focused attention on individual writers and their cognitive abilities, which made consideration of the social—the domain of feminist thought—difficult. In "Composition Studies from a Feminist Perspective," Elizabeth Flynn speculates that the absence of feminist theory in composition studies could have been due to the time-consuming teaching and administrative demands of women in the discipline that make research and publication difficult. She also explains that rhetoric and composition studies emerged after feminist studies, and, as a new and vulnerable discipline, its emphasis was on defining itself rather than on importing outside theories.

5. Of course, this does not mean that the work is not out there. Studies in Rhetorics and Feminism, a series edited by Cheryl Glenn and Shirley Wilson Logan, publishes scholarly works that examine interdisciplinary connections between rhetoric and feminism. Foss, Foss, and Griffin's *Feminist Rhetorical Theories* analyzes the rhetorical strategies employed by individual contemporary feminist writers. The Phelps and Emig collection contains several essays that deal explicitly with feminist rhetoric. Susan Jarratt's influential *Rereading the Sophists* is, of course, a major contributor to ongoing disciplinary conversations about feminist rhetoric, as she argues that the sophistic deconstruction of binaries such as a philosophy/rhetoric and man/woman, as well as the Sophists' "emphasis on habit and practice, on historical contingency, and the rejection of essence" (70), necessarily situate feminist rhetoric as a sophistic rhetoric. JoAnn Campbell's *Toward a Feminist Rhetoric: The Writing of Gertrude Buck* is another example of a historical study that problematizes my earlier assertion that feminism "arrived late" to rhetoric and composition studies. Rae Rosenthal's "Feminists in Action: How to Practice What We Teach" is an example of one teacher's attempt to demonstrate the place of feminist rhetoric in the writing classroom. Assigning feminist writers such as Cixous, Lakoff, Gilligan, and Tompkins, Rosenthal argues that students realize the existence of another kind of scholarly writing, one that is "less combative, definitive, and formulaic and

more anecdotal and questioning than is academic discourse generally. And in the intertextuality and self-referencing of many of these essays, there is a spirit of cooperation, a sense of building upon one another rather than in place of one another" (145). Rosenthal's essay raises the important question: Is there a difference between feminist writing and feminist rhetoric? For my purposes, I argue that the two can overlap but need not be synonymous. For example, it is possible for a feminist to write an essay that does not enact a feminist rhetoric of the sort Rosenthal describes; it is also possible for someone who does not identify as a feminist to deploy the moves described above.

6. Nedra Reynolds further complicates the metaphor of border crossing in her cultural geographic analysis of the material conditions that determine who travels, where, and why. As her research suggests, "[T]he liberating promise of border crossing may only be for those willing to travel. Travel, even the mundane kind, is desirable to those who have the time, access to affordable modes of transport, and either a confident sense of negotiating space or a feeling of safety in new environments" ("Who's Going," 558). Reynolds's research, as well as historical events such as those that occurred on 11 September 2001, emphasize the degree to which the usefulness of border crossing as a metaphor must be contextualized culturally, materially, and historically.

7. Jacqueline Jones Royster argues that the ability of many African American women writers to write in multiple genres is a testament to both their aesthetic talent and their rhetorical prowess (*Traces*, 20). As such, she complicates Freedman's theory, resituating multigenre writing as one of many forms of writing available to these writers.

2. Do I Belong "in" RhetComp?
Revision, Identity, and Multigenre Texts

1. See the section in chapter 1 on "Margins/Borders" for a discussion that problematizes a romanticized version of the borderland metaphor.

2. As David Franke reports in a study of the citation practices in feminist composition, feminist rhetors use what he terms "lateral citation" for precisely the reasons Welch describes. Instead of relying on vertical citations, which set up in order to tear down, feminist rhetors cite other authors as a way of connecting with and building on a shared body of knowledge. As Franke explains, the practice of lateral citation involves writers responding to other writers and joining an ongoing conversation, one in which a speaker's "identity is often established by connection with others rather than argument against them" (376).

3. Patrick Bizzaro uses the language of "not fitting in" as he explores the emotional rhetoric of "narratives of isolation" (240), texts written by those who teach writing on the borders of English studies. He specifically focuses on the pain experienced by those who teach creative writing but whose interest in researching that pedagogy positions them as something other than "real" creative

writers. My argument suggests ways these teachers can combat that isolation (at least within RhetComp) by writing multigenre texts that dramatize their reasons for refusing to position themselves *only* within RhetComp.

3. Putting the Wrong Words Together: Disrupting Narratives in English Studies

1. Recently, while moving, I came upon an old diary that I began in the second grade. I randomly opened it to an entry, which read as follows: "Today I sat on the boys side at lunch." There is no mention of the disruption that ensued.

2. bell hooks argues that fear of losing control of the classroom reflects a professorial investment in maintaining bourgeois decorum (*Teaching*, 188). While my quick decision to return to the girls' side without protest was no doubt tied to Mr. Schenking's authority as male principal, hooks's assertion also demands that I examine the influence of my locations as a white, middle-class, "good-girl" student.

3. For additional assignment examples, see Tom Romano's, *Blending Genre, Altering Style;* and Lillian Bridwell-Bowles's "Experimental Writing."

4. In "The Ambivalence of Reflection," Robert Yagelski problematizes the uncomfortable and troubling consequences of self-reflection, particularly as they affect teachers' levels of self-confidence and abilities to teach well. I agree that good teachers need to feel confident in the classroom. I also believe, however, that the capacity to face hard truths about ourselves *and* change for the better inspires a level of confidence that is much more powerful than if we had never looked hard at ourselves at all.

5. Anne Ruggles Gere makes the excellent point that we need to give students "explicit instruction for using silence strategically in personal writing so that they can deploy it for their own aesthetic, ethical, and political purposes" (219). Her argument encourages me to consider how a student's migration to anther genre might also reflect her/his decision to silence (rather than voice) a transgressive subject position.

6. The student writing reproduced in this essay appears with each author's permission. I have changed their names at their request for purposes of confidentiality.

7. Jeff is a white, 24-year-old student from a working-class background.

8. Examples of Jeff's disdain for the profit motives of universities appear throughout his project. For instance, Jeff describes the university's attempts to persuade him to join its clubs and organizations as follows: "I was getting mail asking me to sign up for scholars' fraternities and 'Red Tassel' and whatever else the school could sell me on."

9. If given the opportunity, I would now ask Jeff if he had considered the fact that his English professors, as members of the campus community, had

access to his weekly column; I personally know several who looked forward to it.

10. One might argue that Jeff's unruliness has not disappeared, that, in fact, his entire project is one big exercise in unruliness. In my initial analyses, I was tempted to think the same. However, given the two-year context within which our teacher-student relationship developed, it is clear to me that in his project Jeff is again demonstrating his rhetorical prowess. By situating himself outside the university communities he disdains, Jeff is aligning himself with his primary audience—me. I do not know if he actually scorns other authorities with the severity his essay demonstrates.

4. Toward Hearing the Impossible: A Multigenre Revision of Robert Connors's "Teaching and Learning as a Man"—Revised

1. See Appendix B for a description of my process rereading an early draft of this chapter. For an explanation of the Burkean reading theory I practiced while rereading this early draft, see Jung, "Burke on Plato, Plato through Burke: Plato Is a Social Constructivist?" Briefly, Burke explains that fragmented, even ideologically opposing, voices can be transformed into unified dialogues through "a process of *transformation* whereby the position at the end transcends the position at the start, so that the position at the start can eventually be seen in terms of the new motivation encountered en route" (*Grammar,* 422, emphasis in original). The key term in this description is *transcend,* which Burke explains as a process through which opposing views cease to be opposing with the adoption of new point of view (*Attitudes,* 336). It is the transcendent term that provides the lens through which this new perspective can be obtained. Interestingly, while the transcendent term is not arrived at until the end of the dialogue, Burke argues that in order for the dialogue to be consistent, the term "must be there at the start, either explicitly or implicitly. Usually it is implicit and is gradually purged of its obscurities" (*Rhetoric of Religion,* 128). Once the transcendent term is located, we can use it to move from a dialectical perspective, one that "leave[s] the competing voices in a jangling relation with one another" to an ultimate perspective, in which there is a "'guiding idea' or 'unitary principle' behind the diversity of voices. The voices would not confront one another as somewhat disrelated competitors that can work together only by the 'mild demoralization' of sheer compromise; rather, they would be like successive positions or moments in a single process" (*Rhetoric of Motives,* 187).

It was through this process of Burkean reading that I landed on the term "relational rhetoric," which is explained in chapter 1 and was used to structure the final multigenre revision of Connors's essay that appears in chapter 4. The idea that revision is most profoundly about relationship was not something I realized until undergoing this reading process; as such, I attribute most of the insights in this book to the work I did in rereading early drafts of chapter 4.

2. I decided to interview male graduate students (rather than male professors) for several reasons. One reason is that I wanted to talk with people who teach undergraduate composition, and most of those people at the University of Arizona are graduate students. Also, I thought I would feel more comfortable talking with my peers; in turn, I thought my peers would be more open with me.

The following is a copy of the memo I distributed:

June 30, 1997
TO: [Teacher's name]
    Male Writing Teacher _____
FR: Julie Jung
    Female Writing Teacher
RE: Will you help me with my diss?
As part of my dissertation research, I want to talk to male writing teachers about their experiences teaching writing to male students. Would you be interested in talking to me about this?

If so, I'd ask you to read before we meet (nervy, aren't I? asking you to read something!) a copy of Robert Connors's "Teaching and Learning as a Man." I'd supply you with a copy of it. It was published in *College English* in 1996. It's a good essay, and I think you'd find it interesting.

My goal is to hear his argument better, and I'm hoping you can help me do that. If you're interested or would like to know more, please fill out the bottom portion of this very business-like memorandum and return it to my mailbox in ML 445. If you're not interested, please recycle. Thanks.

___

Please check one:
___ Fascinating! Of course I'll participate in your study. You can call or email me at . . .
___ I heard you were ABD. So, you've actually started to write? Don't you have to do a proposal first? And isn't this interview business just another avoidance strategy? By the way, I'll talk with you, but you have to buy me coffee or something. Call/email me at . . .
___ This is a feminist plot of some sort. You secretly hate that Connors essay and want to trap me somehow. I need to know more before I can ~~commit~~ agree to read and talk about his essay. Call/email me at . . .
___ [Insert your own message here]

Some of the men who agreed to be interviewed responded to the memo as follows:

"I'd be happy to talk with you—but I'll warn you upfront—two of my least favorite words are 'gender' and 'issues.' PS: I don't answer my phone, but I do return messages."

"Is it okay if I can't/never learned to read?"

"[home phone number], 'cause every chick should get my number. (Ha! Ha!)"

"Who provides the disguise? And if I'm ever a candidate for political office, will my participation in your study surface as to incriminate me?"

5. Teaching and Learning in Relational Spaces

1. Interestingly, Marie is silent about the second moment of confrontation in our class, when I expressed my disappointment to the women-only group. When I asked her to contribute to this chapter, Marie was very busy, having just obtained a new teaching job, so I do not want to read too much into her silence. And yet, I do not want to overlook it, either. As such, I wonder if her silence speaks to her difficulty with reconciling the empowering effects of confrontational pedagogy with other, more painful ones.

2. For more on the dynamics of Freudian transference as they are often played out in the feminist classroom, see Wallace.

3. Ronald Strickland, for example, argues that his version of confrontational pedagogy is "the only way to achieve an intellectually responsible pedagogy" (294). As such, he resists the position of "subject who is supposed to know" only as it relates to course *content*. I am interested in resisting this position in terms of both course content *and* process.

Works Cited

Adams, Kate. "Northamerican Silences: History, Identity, and Witness in the Poetry of Gloria Anzaldúa, Cherríe Moraga, and Leslie Marmon Silko." Hedges and Fisher Fishkin 130–45.

Anzaldúa, Gloria. *Borderlands/La Frontera: The New Mestiza.* San Francisco: Aunt Lute, 1987.

Armstrong, Cherryl. "Reexamining Basic Writing: Lessons from Harvard's Basic Writers." *Journal of Basic Writing* 7 (1988): 68–80.

Bakhtin, M. M. *Speech Genres and Other Late Essays.* Ed. Caryl Emerson and Michael Holquist. Trans. Vern W. McGee. U of Texas Press Slavic Series, no. 8. Austin: U of Texas P, 1986.

Bateson, Mary Catherine. *Composing a Life.* New York: Plume, 1986.

Bawarshi, Anis. "The Genre Function." *College English* 62 (2000): 335–60.

Beach, Richard. "Self-evaluation Strategies of Extensive Revisers and Non-revisers." *College Composition and Communication* 27 (1976): 160–64.

Beach, Richard, and JoAnne Liebman Kleine. "The Writing/Reading Relationship: Becoming One's Own Best Reader." Petersen 64–81.

Behling, Laura L. "'Generic' Multiculturalism: Hybrid Texts, Cultural Contexts." *College English* 65 (2003): 411–26.

Belenky, Mary Field, Blythe McVicker Clinchy, Nancy Rule Goldberger, and Jill Mattuck Tarule. *Women's Ways of Knowing: The Development of Self, Voice, and Mind.* New York: Basic Books, 1986.

Bishop, Wendy. "Suddenly Sexy: Creative Nonfiction Rear-ends Composition." *College English* 65 (2003): 257–75.

Bizarro, Patrick. "Comment: Kostelanetz's Rhetoric of Isolation: Or, Sometimes I Feel Lonely Too." *College English* 64 (2001): 237–42.

Brady, Laura. "The Reproduction of Othering." Jarratt and Worsham 21–44.

Breidenbach, Cathleen. "Comment and Response." *College English* 59 (1997): 470–72.

Bridwell, Lillian S. "Revising Strategies in Twelfth Grade Students' Transactional Writing." *Research in the Teaching of English* 14 (1980): 197–222.

Bridwell-Bowles, Lillian. "Experimental Writing." Conference on College Composition and Communication. Phoenix. 14 March 1997.

———. "Experimental Writing Within the Academy." Phelps and Emig 43–66.

Burke, Kenneth. *Attitudes toward History.* 3rd ed. Berkeley: U of California P, 1984.

————. *A Grammar of Motives.* Berkeley: U of California P, 1969.

————. *Permanence and Change: An Anatomy of Purpose.* 3rd ed. Berkeley: U of California P, 1984.

————. *A Rhetoric of Motives.* Berkeley: U of California P, 1969.

————. *The Rhetoric of Religion: Studies in Logology.* Berkeley: U of California P, 1961.

Butler, Judith. *Gender Trouble: Feminism and the Subversion of Identity.* New York: Routledge, 1990.

Campbell, JoAnn, ed. *Toward a Feminist Rhetoric: The Writing of Gertrude Buck.* Pittsburgh: U of Pittsburgh P, 1996.

Cheung, King-Kok. "Attentive Silence in Joy Kogawa's *Obasan.*" Hedges and Fisher Fishkin 113–29.

Coiner, Constance. "'No One's Private Ground': A Bakhtinian Reading of Tillie Olsen's *Tell Me a Riddle.*" Hedges and Fisher Fishkin 71–93.

Comfort, Juanita Rodgers. "Becoming a Writerly Self: College Writers Engaging Black Feminist Essays." *College Composition and Communication* 51 (2000): 540–59.

Connors, Robert. "Comment and Response." *College English* 58 (1996): 968–74.

————. "Teaching and Learning As a Man." *College English* 58 (1996): 137–57.

Crowley, Sharon, and Debra Hawhee. *Ancient Rhetorics for Contemporary Students.* 2nd ed. Boston: Allyn and Bacon, 1999.

Dallery, Arleen B. "The Politics of Writing (the) Body: Ecriture Feminine." *Theorizing Feminism: Parallel Trends in the Humanities and Social Sciences.* Ed. Anne C. Herrmann and Abigail J. Stewart. Boulder, CO: Westview, 1994. 288–300.

Desser, Daphne. "Reading and Writing the Family: Ethos, Identification, and Identity in My Great-Grandfather's Letters." *Rhetoric Review* 20 (2001): 314–28.

Devitt, Amy J. "Integrating Rhetorical and Literary Theories of Genre." *College English* 62 (2000): 696–718.

Dunn, Patricia A. *Talking, Sketching, Moving: Multiple Literacies in the Teaching of Writing.* Portsmouth, MA: Boynton/Cook, 2001.

DuPlessis, Rachel Blau. *The Pink Guitar: Writing as Feminist Practice.* New York: Routledge, 1990.

Enos, Theresa. *Gender Roles and Faculty Lives in Rhetoric and Composition.* Carbondale: Southern Illinois UP, 1996.

Faigley, Lester. *Fragments of Rationality: Postmodernity and the Subject of Composition.* Pittsburgh: U of Pittsburgh P, 1992.

Faigley, Lester, and Stephen P. Witte. "Analyzing Revision." *College Composition and Communication* 32 (1981): 400–414.

————. "Measuring the Effects of Revisions on Text Structure." *New Directions in Composition Research*. Ed. Richard Beach and Lillian S. Bridwell. New York: Guilford Press, 1987. 95–108.

Farmer, Frank. *Saying and Silence: Listening to Composition with Bakhtin*. Logan: Utah State UP, 2001.

Fitzgerald, Jill. "Research on Revision in Writing." *Review of Educational Research* 57 (1987): 481–506.

————. *Towards Knowledge in Writing: Illustrations from Revision Studies*. New York: Springer, 1992.

Flax, Jane. *Thinking Fragments: Psychoanalysis, Feminism, and Postmodernism in the Contemporary West*. Berkeley: U of California P, 1990.

Flower, Linda, et al. "Detection, Diagnosis and the Strategies of Revision. *College Composition and Communication* 37 (1986): 16–55.

Flynn, Elizabeth. "Composing as a Woman." *College Composition and Communication* 39 (1988): 423–35.

————. "Composition from a Feminist Perspective." *The Politics of Writing Instruction, Postsecondary*. Ed. Richard H. Bullock and John Trimbur. Portsmouth, MA: Boynton/Cook, 1991. 137–54.

————. "Review: Feminist Theories/Feminist Composition." *College English* 57 (1995): 201–12.

Flynn, Elizabeth, and Patrocinio P. Schweickart, eds. *Gender and Reading: Essays on Readers, Texts, and Contexts*. Baltimore: John Hopkins UP, 1986.

Foss, Karen A., Sonja K. Foss, and Cindy L. Griffin, eds. *Feminist Rhetorical Theories*. Thousand Oaks, CA: Sage, 1999.

Foucault, Michel. *Power/Knowledge: Selected Interviews and Other Writings 1972–1977*. Ed. Colin Gordon. Trans. Colin Gordon, et al. New York: Pantheon, 1980.

Franke, David. "Writing into Unmapped Territory: The Practice of Lateral Citation." Phelps and Emig 375–84.

Freedman, Diane P. *An Alchemy of Genres: Cross-Genre Writing by American Feminist Poet-Critics*. Charlottesville: U of Virginia P, 1992.

Garoian, Charles R. *Performing Pedagogy: Toward an Art of Politics*. Albany: State U of New York P, 1999.

Geertz, Clifford. "Blurred Genres: The Refiguration of Social Thought." *American Scholar* 49 (1980): 165–82.

Gere, Anne Ruggles. "Revealing Silence: Rethinking Personal Writing." *College Composition and Communication* 53 (2001): 203–23.

Gilligan, Carol. *In a Different Voice: Psychological Theory and Women's Development*. Cambridge: Harvard UP, 1982.

Greenbaum, Andrea. "'Bitch Pedagogy': Agonistic Discourse and the Politics of Resistance." *Insurrections: Approaches to Resistance in Composition Studies*. Ed. Andrea Greenbaum. Albany: State U of New York P, 2001. 151–68.

Hassett, Michael. "Increasing Response-ability through Mortification: A Burkean Perspective on the Teaching of Writing." *JAC* 15 (1995): 471–88.

Hedges, Elaine, and Shelley Fisher Fishkin, eds. *Listening to Silences: New Essays in Feminist Criticism.* New York: Oxford UP, 1994.

Hindman, Jane E. "Making Writing Matter: Using 'the Personal' to Recover[y] an Essential[ist] Tension in Academic Discourse." *College English* 64 (2001): 88–108.

hooks, bell. *Teaching to Transgress: Education as the Practice of Freedom.* New York: Routledge, 1994.

———. "Toward a Revolutionary Feminist Pedagogy." *Talking Back: Thinking Feminist, Thinking Black.* Boston: South End Press, 1989. 49–54.

Janangelo, Joseph. "Joseph Cornell and the Artistry of Composing Persuasive Hypertexts." *College Composition and Communication* 49 (1998): 24–44.

Jarratt, Susan C. "Feminism in Composition: The Case for Conflict." *Contending with Words: Composition and Rhetoric in a Postmodern Age.* Ed. Patricia Harkin and John Schilb. New York: MLA, 1991. 105–23.

———. *Rereading the Sophists: Classical Rhetoric Refigured.* Carbondale: Southern Illinois UP, 1991.

Jarratt, Susan C., and Lynn Worsham, eds. *Feminism and Composition Studies: In Other Words.* New York: MLA, 1998.

Jung, Julie. "Burke on Plato, Plato through Burke: Plato Is a Social Constructivist?" *Composition Studies* 24 (Spring-Fall 1996): 111–24.

Kirsch, Gesa E. "Comment and Response." *College English* 58 (1996): 966–68.

———. "Review: Feminist Critical Pedagogy and Composition." *College English* 57 (1995): 723–29.

———. *Women Writing the Academy: Audience, Authority, and Transformation.* Carbondale: Southern Illinois UP, 1993.

Lamb, Catherine E. "Beyond Argument in Feminist Composition." *College Composition and Communication* 42 (1991): 11–24.

Linn, Ray. *A Teacher's Introduction to Postmodernism.* Urbana, IL: NCTE, 1996.

Lu, Min-Zhan. "Reading and Writing Differences: The Problematic of Experience." Jarratt and Worsham 239–51.

———. "Reading the Personal: Critical Trajectories." *College English* 64 (2001): 52–55.

———. "Redefining the Literate Self: The Politics of Critical Affirmation" *College Composition and Communication* 51 (1999): 172–94.

Luke, Carmen, and Jennifer Gore, eds. *Feminisms and Critical Pedagogies.* New York: Routledge, 1992.

Lynch, Dennis A., Diane George, and Marilyn M. Cooper. "Moments of Argument: Agonistic Inquiry and Confrontational Cooperation." *College Composition and Communication* 48 (1997): 61–85.

Mairs, Nancy. "In Search Of 'In Search of Our Mothers' Gardens': Alice Walker."

Reprinted in *Writing as Re-Vision: A Student's Anthology.* Ed. Beth Alvarado and Barbara Cully. Needham Heights, MA: Simon and Schuster, 1996. 630–35.

———. *Voice Lessons: On Becoming a (Woman) Writer.* Boston: Beacon Press, 1994.

Malinowitz, Harriet. "Business, Pleasure, and the Personal Essay." *College English* 65 (2003): 305–22.

Matsuhashi, A., and E. Gordon. "Revision, Addition, and the Power of the Unseen Text." *The Acquisition of Written Language: Response and Revision.* Ed. S. Freedman. Norwood, NJ: Ablex, 1985. 226–49.

McGann, Patrick. "Comment and Response." *College English* 58 (1996): 964–66.

Micciche, Laura R. "Male Plight and Feminist Threat in Composition Studies: A Response to 'Teaching and Learning as a Man.'" *Composition Studies* 25 (1997): 21–36.

Miller, Jane. *Working Time: Essays on Poetry, Culture, and Travel.* Ann Arbor: U of Michigan P, 1992.

Miller, Nancy K. *Getting Personal: Feminist Occasions and Other Autobiographical Acts.* New York: Routledge, 1991.

Miller, Richard E. "The Nervous System." *College English* 58 (1996): 265–86.

Murray, Donald. *Expecting the Unexpected: Teaching Myself—and Others—to Read and Write.* Upper Montclair, NJ: Boynton/Cook, 1989.

———. "Internal Revision: A Process of Discovery." *Research on Composing: Points of Departure.* Ed. Charles R. Cooper and Lee Odell. Urbana, IL: NCTE, 1978. 85–103.

Newton, Judith, and Judith Stacey. "Ms.Representations: Reflections on Studying Academic Men." *Women Writing Culture.* Ed. Ruth Behar and Deborah A. Gordon. Berkeley: U of California P, 1995. 287–305.

North, Stephen M., et al. *Refiguring the Ph.D. in English Studies: Writing, Doctoral Education, and the Fusion-Based Curriculum.* Urbana, IL: NCTE, 2000.

Olsen, Tillie. *Silences: Classic Essays in the Art of Creating.* New York: Delta, 1978.

Ostergarrd, Lori Alden. "Rethinking Delivery: The (Hyper)Hysterical Text and the Mind/Body Split." www.ilstu.edu/~laoster/newstarthere.htm. Nov. 21, 2004.

Perl, Sondra. "The Composing Processes of Unskilled College Writers." *Research in the Teaching of English* 13 (1979): 317–36.

Petersen, Bruce T., ed. *Convergences: Transactions in Reading and Writing.* Urbana, IL: NCTE, 1986.

Phelps, Louise Wetherbee, and Janet Emig, eds. *Feminine Principles and Women's Experience in American Composition and Rhetoric.* Pittsburgh: U of Pittsburgh P, 1995.

Pratt, Mary Louise. "Arts of the Contact Zone." *Profession* (1991): 33–40.

Qualley, Donna. *Turns of Thought: Teaching Composition as Reflexive Inquiry.* Portsmouth, MA: Boynton/Cook, 1997.

Ratcliffe, Krista. "Rhetorical Listening: A Trope for Interpretive Invention and a 'Code of Cross-Cultural Conduct.'" *College Composition and Communication* 51 (1999): 195–224.

Reynolds, Nedra. "Interrupting Our Way to Agency: Feminist Cultural Studies and Composition." Jarratt and Worsham 58–73.

———. "Who's Going to Cross This Border? Travel Metaphors, Material Conditions, and Contested Places." *JAC* 20 (2000): 541–64.

Ritchie, Joy, and Kate Ronald. "Riding Long Coattails, Subverting Tradition: The Tricky Business of Feminists Teaching Rhetoric(s)." Jarratt and Worsham 217–38.

Romano, Tom. *Blending Genre, Altering Style: Writing Multigenre Papers.* Portsmouth, MA: Boynton/Cook, 2000.

Rosenthal, Rae. "Feminists in Action: How to Practice What We Teach." *Left Margins: Cultural Studies and Composition Pedagogy.* Ed. Karen Fitts and Alan France. Albany: State U of New York P, 1995. 139–56.

Rouzie, Albert. "Beyond the Dialectic of Work and Play: A Serio-Ludic Rhetoric for Composition Studies." *JAC* 20 (2000): 627–58.

Royster, Jacqueline Jones. *Traces of a Stream: Literacy and Social Change Among African American Women.* Pittsburgh: U of Pittsburgh P, 2000.

———. "When the First Voice You Hear Is Not Your Own." *College Composition and Communication* 47 (1996): 29–40.

Schweickart, Patricinio. "Reading Ourselves: Toward a Feminist Theory of Reading." Flynn and Schweickart 31–62.

Sommers, Nancy. "Revision Strategies of Student Writers and Experienced Adult Writers." *College Composition and Communication* 31 (1980): 378–88.

Strickland, Ronald. "Confrontationl Pedagogy and Traditional Literary Studies." *College English* 52 (1990): 291–300.

Van Dyne, Susan R. *Revising Life: Sylvia Plath's Ariel Poems.* Chapel Hill: U of North Carolina P, 1993.

Walker, Nancy A. *The Disobedient Writer: Women and Narrative Tradition.* Austin: U of Texas P, 1995.

Wall, Susan V. "Rereading the Discourses of Gender in Composition: A Cautionary Tale." *Pedagogy in the Age of Politics: Writing and Reading (in) the Academy.* Ed. Patricia Sullivan and Donna J. Qualley. Urbana, IL: NCTE, 1994. 166–82.

Wallace, Miriam L. "Beyond Love and Battle: Practicing Feminist Pedagogy." *Feminist Teacher* 12 (1999): 184–98.

Weedon, Chris. *Feminist Practice and Poststructuralist Theory.* Cambridge, MA: Blackwell, 1987.

Welch, Nancy. *Getting Restless: Rethinking Revision in Writing Instruction.* Portsmouth, MA: Boynton/Cook, 1997.

———. "Playing with Reality: Writing Centers and the Mirror Stage." *College Composition and Communication* 51 (1999): 51–69.

———. "Sideshadowing Teacher Response." *College English* 60 (1998): 374–95.

Yagelski, Robert P. "The Ambivalence of Reflection." *College Composition and Communication* 51 (1999): 32–50.

Index

Julie Jung is an assistant professor of English at Illinois State University, where she teaches courses in rhetorical theory, composition theory, and writing, with an emphasis on theories and practices of revision. Her publications have appeared in *JAC*, *Composition Studies*, and *Living Languages: Contexts for Reading and Writing*. Currently she is working on an edited collection that investigates issues unique to teaching and learning English at the graduate level.

Studies in Writing & Rhetoric

In 1980 the Conference on College Composition and Communication established the Studies in Writing & Rhetoric (SWR) series as a forum for monograph-length arguments or presentations that engage general compositionists. SWR encourages extended essays or research reports addressing any issue in composition and rhetoric from any theoretical or research perspective as long as the general significance to the field is clear. Previous SWR publications serve as models for prospective authors; in addition, contributors may propose alternate formats and agendas that inform or extend the field's current debates.

SWR is particularly interested in projects that connect the specific research site or theoretical framework to contemporary classroom and institutional contexts of direct concern to compositionists across the nation. Such connections may come from several approaches, including cultural, theoretical, field-based, gendered, historical, and interdisciplinary. SWR especially encourages monographs by scholars early in their careers, by established scholars who wish to share an insight or exhortation with the field, and by scholars of color.

The SWR series editor and editorial board members are committed to working closely with prospective authors and offering significant developmental advice for encouraged manuscripts and prospectuses. Editorships rotate every five years. Prospective authors intending to submit a prospectus during the 2002 to 2007 editorial appointment should obtain submission guidelines from Robert Brooke, SWR editor, University of Nebraska–Lincoln, Department of English, P.O. Box 880337, 202 Andrews Hall, Lincoln, NE 68588-0337.

General inquiries may also be addressed to Sponsoring Editor, Studies in Writing & Rhetoric, Southern Illinois University Press, P.O. Box 3697, Carbondale, IL 62902-3697.